Sell Your Art or Not?

Malcolm Dewey

Copyright

Table of Contents

Dedication

To Kerrin and the boys My daily motivation

Blurb

I wrote this book for you

Are you an artist wondering if it's time to take your creative talents from a cherished hobby to a thriving side hustle or even a full-time career? "Sell Your Art or Not?" is your guide to making this life-changing decision confidently and clearly.

In this book, you'll explore the key considerations, pros, and cons of turning your artistic passion into a profitable venture. Whether you're contemplating selling your art part-time or dreaming of becoming a full-time artist, this book provides the insights and advice you need to navigate the transition.

Discover invaluable tips on:

The Arguments for Going Pro or Staying a Hobbyist: What will be best for you?

Marketing Your Art: Learn effective strategies to promote your work and reach your ideal audience.

Working with Galleries: Understand the dynamics of gallery representation and how to build successful partnerships.

Handling Commissions: Gain practical advice on managing commissions and custom projects.

Legal Aspects: Get informed about the legalities of selling art, including contracts, copyrights, and taxes.

Work-Life Balance: Find out how to maintain a healthy balance between your creative pursuits and personal life.

and more

Drawing from my personal journey and experiences, "Sell Your Art or Not?" offers a blend of inspiration, practical guidance, and real-world examples. This book is designed for every creative individual who has ever dreamed of making something more out of their passion for art. By the end, you'll have the knowledge and confidence to decide about your artistic future.

Take the first step towards transforming your art into a fulfilling and successful endeavor. "Sell Your Art or Not?" is here to help you navigate your creative path with wisdom and insight.

A Decision that I Will Never Regret

Do you sell your art or not? That is a simple question to answer. Except it isn't. It turns out that because we are human, this question can open up a deep and confusing rabbit hole for us to dive into. Most artists are happy to admit that if someone wants to buy one of their paintings, they will agree to sell it. A little extra money can be used for many things. More paints, for instance. That is good. However, it is not long before our thoughts turn to selling our art regularly. What then? A side hustle that brings in a regular income. Nice. Then, the side hustle begins to grow. Sales increase, and you start getting more positive feedback. Could this become something more? Do you dream that life as a full-time artist is possible? What now?

You may not need to go through this long process. Maybe you are ready to go fulltime now. Would you like to know if this will be a huge mistake? You may be confident about your quality of work. It is just the mechanics of making this dream come true. What to do? Now, we can see that the title is not that simple to answer. I discovered this for myself, and this book is my way of answering the many questions. I went through a long and careful transition from one career to another. It worked out better than I had ever dreamed possible. Hopefully, you can answer some of your questions or, at least, get a little more light shining down that rabbit hole. To help set the scene, let me tell you my story. Don't worry, I have edited out the boring bits, and there are no slides either.

When I was at school, I loved painting, drawing, and sketching. I've been doing that since a very early age, and a sketchbook was my constant companion. I kept up this process throughout my primary school years, and in high school, I got the opportunity to study art with an art school that was contracted to my high school.

These were three wonderful years. I could spend the afternoons at the art school painting, and they also taught us art theory. I was exposed to the world of artists. These were teachers outside the typical school system, and a sense of freedom and fun was part of the learning process.

Or perhaps it was simply because I enjoyed art so much that this was such a wonderful way to spend my time. Even though I was a student and had to write tests and exams, none of this mattered. Art was always considered to be simple, and I could handle it without much trouble.

I also discovered Impressionism through art theory classes and realized that this art movement suited my personality. Today, I consider myself a contemporary Impressionist painter.

A lot has happened between then and now. Some of that has prompted me to write this book because I know many artists, perhaps yourself, are trying to decide what to do with their lives. Should art feature more prominently as a way to make an extra income? Can art become more than that?

There have been quite a few dramatic changes in my life. At school, I studied graphic design. That involved designing posters and book covers, coming up with art concepts, and doing lettering as well. It was kind of like Toulouse-Lautrec, the nineteenth-century artist who created wonderful posters—except without the absinthe and can-can dancers.

I wasn't doing fine art like I am doing today. In any case, when I went to vocational classes, which were designed to help final-year high school students decide what direction they wanted to take, where they were going to study, and what possible careers lay ahead, I obviously went to all the talks on art.

However, no one has talked about art as a career in fine art. It was things like fashion design or textile design. That was about it.

Of those two, I guess textile design was the closest to what I could look forward to, which wasn't particularly exciting to me. Although, of course, with hindsight, much has changed in the world. You can certainly have a very fulfilling and purposeful career with everything that goes into textile design and lifestyle design these days. This was back in the 80s, so it was either that or becoming a starving artist.

So what did I do? Of course, I opted to study law at university, the natural choice—with tongue firmly in cheek. I enjoy languages, history, English, and content subjects. Studying from books was simple, and law is all about studying from books. So I went off to university, had a great time, and emerged after five years with a Bachelor of Laws degree. Then, I did my articles of clerkship with a law firm, wrote the exams, was admitted as a fully qualified attorney, and was employed as a young lawyer. After a few years, due to changes in my situation, I got an opportunity to join a partnership with another lawyer. This was a horrific decision for me and led to about six years of struggle and conflict.

Let me say whatever you've heard about partnerships and how miserable they can be, it's true. Avoid them if you can. In any event, that was my experience of partnerships. That time was not all bad, though, because I got married.

We met during my first employment as a young attorney. She was employed in the legal secretarial department, and of course, I struck up a relationship with this rather cute secretary. It was so typical. But we were similar ages, and we were meant to be. A few years later, and stuck in the horrible partnership, we decided to get married and get on with our lives. We had our children during these six years of professional misery. Real highlights. The funny thing is we were poor, in debt, and facing enormous challenges, but we jumped into the deep end and started swimming. When you are in your twenties, you grab life by the horns.

So there were definite highlights, and we also had a lot of fun in our personal lives. But things came to a head, and I had to make a decision. I terminated the partnership and started my own law practice. Shortly thereafter, my wife joined me as an office manager, and what followed was about seventeen years of running and managing my legal practice with the capable assistance of my wife.

During this time, we also partly homeschooled our children. When I think back on how we had time for anything, it's pretty astonishing. But when you're young, you make a way. The excuse of not having time was never an option. We had to knuckle down, so we found the time.

During this period, let's say ten years into this business venture, which was doing very well and was very busy, I made a decision that had far-ranging consequences. The cliche "little did he know" applies to this one.

It was a public holiday, and I spent the day with my family. On a whim I picked up a piece of paper and some pastels that belonged to my children and did a painting. It was the first bit of art I had tried in years, and I enjoyed it so much. My wife was impressed, too. We even had it framed. It was a pretty lousy piece of art, but it started to open the floodgates or at least cause a few cracks in the floodgates. I got some acrylic paints the following weekend and started painting.

That painting was very enjoyable, and not too bad, either. I also discovered I wasn't interested in graphic design anymore. I wanted to paint like an impressionist.

One thing led to another, and this growing hobby became a compulsion. We made space in our bedroom for a tiny studio, just an easel where I could paint, and my wife encouraged me. And that's what I did, painted away.

By the end of that year, I had exhibited some paintings at a Christmas market in our town and sold a few. My first painting sold was a picture of a lighthouse, done with a painting knife. It was quite bold and colorful. Well, that started things off.

I spent the next six years growing this side hustle. I started a website, I started blogging, and I started looking for places to hang my paintings. Local restaurants were a popular way to get your paintings before the eyes of potential buyers.

I would take part in local markets, flea markets, thrift markets, all these sorts of things where you could just put up a table and set out your paintings. I did that whenever I could, because I had the time on a Saturday and Sunday.

I also studied. I studied like a bookworm because that's basically what I am. I watched videos, went to workshops, and absorbed as much information as possible, trying to put that into practice. I painted every day, as far as possible, in the afternoons or evenings, and on the weekends.

And I grew this side hustle into leading a double life. Mornings as an attorney running an office. I had some young attorneys helping me to manage this busy practice so that I could break out the paints in the afternoons.

This led to recording lessons to start a YouTube channel. I was doing all the things that I felt I had to do because the aim was to hit the ground running as a full-time artist when the time was right. As I said, I spent six years building this up, much to my wife's credit for sticking it out for all that time because she wanted us to get out much sooner while we still had our sanity.

Our children had to finish school. A lot was going on—a lot of stress.

Could we survive without the law practice? Could we provide for ourselves? Could we provide for our children if they wanted to go to university? Could we do all of these things and survive? Well, I always believed in one thing: We would never be allowed to starve. We would always have food on the table. So, with that in mind, we put up a house for sale and parceled the law practice off to other lawyers.

I just gave the business away over about twelve months. That was how determined and confident we were. Or should I say, just determined and confident enough to take our chances?

And things worked out. We sold our house, moved to a small seaside town, and I set up a painting studio, created workshops, started online teaching, and painted like crazy.

I think I've painted buckets and buckets of paint over the years, quite an astonishing amount, to build up my painting ability. That was the only way I knew to do so: work as hard as possible and build that up. The moment we committed to life as a full-time artist, I saw the art business grow at a rapid pace, which proved to me that I could survive.

I could even thrive with art today, with the internet, of course, and being able to reach people worldwide. We live in a small town, a small country, and it has a very small art market, probably as big as one city in the United States, for example. So, I realized I had to think globally and reach people worldwide, and that's what I set out to do.

I'm happy to say that it has worked out for me. Perhaps it was a bit of luck and good fortune, but most of all, it was a lot of work. You've got to put in the time and effort, and you've got to love what you do.

If you love what you do, it makes it so much easier. I've never got up in the morning and thought, oh dear, another day of the art business. Instead, I've loved every minute of it.

I can assure you that it is a stark difference from being a full-time lawyer. So that was it. The transition process did work.

It was how I could hit the ground running and not disappoint anyone. I was not going to start an art business and have my family suffer. I'm just not wired that way.

So, I had to hit the ground running. Of course, I did save money to help with that. I needed at least 12 months' emergency fund, and we killed off all credit card debt.

Common sense things like that make big changes like this possible. So, with all of that behind me and many years now as a full-time artist, I can hopefully contribute something to this book that will be helpful to you if you have similar plans. Or perhaps you want to work on a side hustle.

That is also an excellent way to work. I can share some of my tips, experiences, and suggestions, which may be helpful to you. So, with that out of the way, let's dive into the book and see if you can decide whether to turn your hobby into an art business.

The Argument to Remain a Hobby Painter

Let us deal with the elephant in the room. It is not fair to pump up the idea of turning your art into a side hustle or full-time career without considering the counter-argument. Transitioning into a full-time art career can be incredibly rewarding, but it is not the right path for everyone. There are compelling reasons for hobby artists to remain amateurs, maintaining their secure jobs or pensions while enjoying art as a fulfilling hobby. Here's why this argument is persuasive for many:

1. **Financial Stability and Security**:

Regular Paycheck: A traditional job provides a steady income, which is often more predictable and stable than an art career's fluctuating earnings.

Benefits and Retirement: Many traditional jobs offer benefits like health insurance, retirement plans, and paid leave, which are not typically available to freelance artists.

Economic Uncertainty: The art market can be volatile and unpredictable. Keeping a stable job mitigates the financial risks associated with trying to earn a living solely from art.

Emergency Fund: A secure job ensures a financial cushion for emergencies, which can be harder to maintain when relying on inconsistent art sales.

2. Freedom from Pressure

Creative Freedom: No Commercial Constraints: As a hobbyist, you can create purely for personal satisfaction without the pressure to conform to market trends or client demands.

Exploration and Experimentation: Without the need to sell, you have the freedom to experiment with different styles, mediums, and subjects without worrying about marketability.

Avoiding Burnout: The pressure to constantly produce, market, and sell art can lead to burnout. Maintaining art as a hobby helps preserve your passion and enjoyment.

Mental Well-being: Managing a business, meeting deadlines, and dealing with financial uncertainties can be draining on mental health. Keeping art as a hobby can maintain it as a source of relaxation and joy.

3. Balanced Lifestyle

Time Management: Balancing a full-time art career with your personal life can be challenging. Retaining a traditional job provides a clear separation between work and leisure.

Family and Social Life: Maintaining a secure job allows more predictable hours, leaving ample time for family, friends, and other interests.

Personal Fulfillment: A fulfilling hobby allows you to pursue other interests and passions without monetizing them. This can lead to a more well-rounded and satisfying life.

Purpose and Satisfaction: Many people find purpose and satisfaction in their traditional careers that complement their artistic pursuits. Art remains a source of personal fulfillment rather than a job.

4. Reduced Business Responsibilities

Less Bureaucracy: Running an art business involves a significant amount of administrative work, including accounting, marketing, and legal responsibilities. As a hobbyist, you avoid these tasks.

Focus on Creation: Without the burden of business management, you can devote more time and energy to creating art.

Marketing and Sales: Marketing yourself and your work can be daunting and time-consuming. Staying a hobbyist means you don't have to engage in constant self-promotion.

Rejection and Criticism: The commercial artist faces potential rejection and criticism, which can be discouraging. As a hobbyist, you can avoid this aspect and focus on the positive aspects of creating.

5. Realistic Assessment of Commitment and Skills

Honest Self-Evaluation: Many hobby artists may be unwilling to commit the time and effort required to turn their art into a business. It's crucial to be honest about your willingness to undertake this journey.

Skill Development: Developing the skills necessary to compete in the art market takes time and dedication. If you're not fully committed to this growth, enjoying art as a hobby may be better.

Personal Goals: Understanding why you create art is essential. If your primary goal is personal satisfaction and enjoyment, there's no need to turn it into a career.

Long-Term Vision: Consider your long-term vision for your life and career. If you value security and stability more than an art career's challenges and potential rewards, staying a hobbyist is wise.

Many of us can relate to keeping art as a hobby rather than transitioning to a full-time career. This path allows for financial stability, creative freedom, and a balanced lifestyle without the pressures and risks of the art market. It enables us to enjoy our craft purely for the joy it brings, maintaining it as a fulfilling and stress-free part of our lives. You must carefully consider your personal goals, commitment levels, and the realities of the art business to determine your best path.

I'm still determined to carry on, you say? Well, let us dig a little deeper.

The Argument in Favor of Selling Your Art

When considering the decision to sell your art, whether as a side hustle or as a full-time career, it's essential to address the common concerns and counterarguments that suggest keeping art purely as a hobby. Selling your art has many benefits. Let us examine these in greater detail.

Financial Benefits

Side Hustle Potential: Selling art as a side hustle can provide a valuable source of supplementary income. This additional cash can help cover bills, fund art supplies, or be saved for future projects. Did you know that even a modest sum added towards paying down debt can save a bundle in interest payments over time? This was one of my early motivations when we were paying off a mortgage bond. Even a little extra money to pay for new art materials removes any guilt about spending money on art supplies. You get the point- a little extra dough never goes amiss.

Full-Time Career: Transitioning to a full-time art career can be financially rewarding for those with a strong passion and dedication. Many artists successfully earn a living through their craft. I do, and in the beginning, I honestly did not think that would be the case. Aside from making a living, you can also improve your lifestyle. Honestly, who needs a stressful commute each day, a soul-sucking job and more stress getting home after sunset? Lost family time and lack of purpose in life. If this is your life, making a plan B seems like a good idea.

Investment in Your Art

The money earned from selling your art can be reinvested into your artistic practice, allowing you to purchase better materials, attend workshops, or expand your studio space. Investing in yourself benefits yourself and your loved ones, who can see how happy your creativity makes you.

Validation and Recognition

Selling your art helps you reach a broader audience and gain public recognition. Building an audience is a term used to describe this, but I like to think of it as growing your support among like-minded friends. Positive feedback and sales can validate your talent and efforts. Your confidence grows, and your sense of purpose grows, too.

Networking Opportunities: Engaging with buyers and other artists can open doors to exhibitions, collaborations, and commissions. You can compare this to a giant waterwheel. As the trickle of water gains and grows and adds greater weight to the wheel, the wheel gradually begins to turn. Once the big wheel begins to turn and the water keeps flowing, the wheel speeds up. Now, it is turning easily on its momentum. In the same way, your efforts are rewarded on an ever-increasing basis.

Confidence Boost

Artistic Validation: Knowing someone values your work enough to purchase it can significantly boost your confidence and encourage you to continue developing your skills. I can still remember that first sale. It gave me a huge confidence boost. If I could sell that painting to a stranger, then why not another one? Now that I knew what people liked, I could create paintings in that general style and probably sell more at the next market. That is, as it happens, how things worked out.

3. Personal Growth and Development

Goal Setting: Selling your art provides concrete goals to work towards, such as completing a series for an exhibition or meeting a commission deadline. This can increase your productivity and drive. A talent I learned as an attorney was to let deadlines motivate me. Most attorneys work that way. The last-minute dash and adrenalin rush is how most things get done in a law firm. As an artist, I know this can work, too, but why create stress? Now I love my work and mostly get my art or writing done quickly. A little every day does add up to a lot over time.

Continuous Learning: Marketing and selling your art requires learning new skills, such as business management, marketing, and networking, contributing to your overall personal development. It is nice to know that you are not only a consumer but also a creator. You contribute positively to the world. You get to use exciting tools, whether analog or digital, and make things happen.

Professionalism and Career Development: Treating your art as a business, even a side hustle, helps you develop a professional mindset. This includes improving your time management, financial planning, and strategic thinking. You grow as a person. You transform yourself for the better.

4. Impact and Influence

Cultural Contribution: Selling your art allows you to share your unique perspective and contribute to the cultural landscape. Your work can inspire, provoke thought, and bring joy to others. I believe this to be true. It is not merely an artsy-fartsy fantasy. I am unashamedly trying to add a little beauty to the world. I surround myself with beauty in my home. I wish more people would do the same to their own living spaces. I am saddened when I walk into someone's home to find bare walls everywhere.

Legacy Building: Selling your art creates a lasting legacy. Your pieces can be passed down through generations. Who knows? No one until they try. Your work could be displayed in public and private collections. Naturally, only some of us will reach those heady heights, and it need not be your goal, but if it is, then go for it.

Engaging with Others: Selling your art fosters connections with other artists, collectors, and enthusiasts. These relationships can provide support, inspiration, and collaboration opportunities. They also make your day! Is it not wonderful to bring joy into other people's lives just by creating art? I think it is a superpower.

Building a Community: Your art can create a community of followers who share your passion and support your work, providing a sense of belonging and mutual appreciation. I love this, too. It is profoundly rewarding to see artists, inspired by my art classes, creating and talking about their art to other artists. Thinking that I had a hand in starting a positive conversation with others is very important to me. You can do this through your art and becoming an advocate for creative arts.

5. Flexibility and Autonomy

Creative Freedom: Selling your art allows you to pursue your creative vision while controlling your career path. You choose what to create, how to market it, and whom to sell it to.

Work-Life Balance: As a full-time artist, you can set your schedule, choose your projects, and balance your work with personal life commitments. My life changed dramatically from office commitments, multitudes of red tape, and having to attend numerous client meetings. When I opened my studio as a full-time artist, it was just me. No meetings, no phone ringing, no clients to meet, no red tape, no worries about whether I had a court appearance that I somehow forgot to diarise. Nothing but me in a studio with paints and canvas. Since that happy day, I have added many things to do—painting, writing, video days, editing days, planning new tutorials, posting to social media, and so on. All of which is a joy to do.

Multiple Streams of Income: Selling art opens up various income opportunities, such as commissions, prints, licensing deals, teaching, and workshops. This diversification can provide financial stability and creative variety. It takes time, energy, bravery, and showing up for work. All of it is fun to do. You decide your schedule and do what you can. The beautiful part is that what you produce brings joy to many people. At worst, it does not offend anyone. Compared to that stressful desk job, the choice is simple to make.

6. Addressing Concerns About "Selling Out"

Authentic Expression: Selling your art does not mean compromising your artistic integrity. Many successful artists create work that is both commercially viable and personally meaningful.

Setting Boundaries: You can set boundaries to remain true to your vision. Choose projects and clients that align with your values and artistic goals. On this note, be careful about taking on commissions. In my experience, it is the sense of obligation to accept a commission that leads to problems. If the client, subject, and commission terms are not to your liking, you will almost certainly run into issues. This can create a sour note in your life, which, with hindsight, you did not need. I have often asked myself why I took on that commission. It has caused me too much grief. I know the answer, though. Ego, the desire for income, and the idea that I have something to add to my resume. However, the client was difficult, and I underpriced myself because I was not confident, and the subject was a bore to paint. Lesson learned.

A variation on the theme is when a collector says that they love your painting of XYZ, but can you do it bigger and in some other colors that will match their decor? The answer is ... It is up to you. Does the request upset you? Then, it is best that you pass on the offer. If the request is easy-peasy and you are keen as houses to jump in, then go for it. I let my gut instinct guide me as far as possible. You don't need to accept the offer right away. Consider it overnight. Make a decision that you are happy with, and be true to yourself.

Commissions are a topic all on their own and are not the subject of this book. However, research the ins and outs. Get everything in writing, and if you accept a commission, give it your best effort.

Outdated Notion: The idea of "selling out" is increasingly outdated. Many artists balance commercial success with artistic integrity in today's art world. Nobody has the right to suggest that you should not make a sound, honest living from your art.

Empowerment: Selling your art empowers you to make a living from your passion, which can be a deeply fulfilling and liberating experience.

Whether as a side hustle or a full-time career, selling your art offers numerous benefits, including financial rewards, personal growth, public recognition, and professional development. While it comes with challenges, the opportunity to share your work, inspire others, and gain financial independence can make it a highly rewarding endeavor. By balancing commercial success and artistic integrity, you can create a fulfilling and sustainable art practice that enriches both your life and the lives of others.

Deciding Whether to Pursue Art as a Profession

You have considered the arguments and still want to go ahead. Let us carefully consider several factors when deciding whether to pursue art as a profession or keep it as a hobby. This chapter will explore these factors and discuss the importance of evaluating your skills, goals, and personal circumstances to make an informed decision. Let us accept that you live and breathe art. Life as an artist is your calling. What next? Evaluating your skills is the next step towards making a decision. Take the time to assess your artistic abilities objectively. Consider your technical skills, creativity, and style. Are you skilled enough to produce quality artwork that can be sold? I am not saying it has to be great art. You do not need to be a master at creating jaw-dropping work. Not at all. You do, however, need to be at a level that does suggest something beyond hobbyist. Vague, I know, but categorizing art this way is difficult.

Do you have the makings of a style that sets you apart from other artists? You do not need to settle on a style. It is more like having a vision of where you want to take your painting. Vision is super important in my opinion. Style is ever-changing, but creative vision is powerful and will sustain you over the long haul. Evaluating these aspects will help you gauge whether your art has the potential for commercial success. Seeking feedback is also crucial during this evaluation process. Show your work to trusted friends, fellow artists, or even art professionals for constructive criticism. They can provide valuable insights on areas where you excel and areas needing improvement. Please remember that feedback should be seen as an opportunity for growth rather than criticism. Setting artistic goals is another important aspect of deciding whether to pursue art professionally. Take some time to define your artistic aspirations and establish achievable targets. Do you want to gain recognition in the art world? Do you dream of having solo exhibitions or being represented by galleries? Setting clear goals will help guide your artistic journey and provide motivation along the way. It is that notion of having a vision rearing its head once again. However, it's important to focus on both long-term and short-term goals. Break down larger aspirations into smaller milestones that can be achieved within a reasonable timeframe. This approach allows for a sense of accomplishment and keeps motivation levels high. What can be done today, next week, and in a month? While evaluating skills and setting goals are essential steps in deciding whether to sell your art or keep it as a hobby, personal circumstances cannot be ignored either. Your financial stability plays a significant role in determining if pursuing art professionally is feasible. Consider whether you have a stable income source or if you'll need to rely solely on your art sales for financial support. Can you put aside an emergency fund? More on these aspects later. Time commitment is another crucial factor to consider. Pursuing art professionally requires a considerable amount of time and effort. Do you have the time to dedicate to creating art consistently, marketing your work, and managing the business side of being an artist? Assessing your availability will help determine if you can make the necessary commitments. Personal obligations such as family responsibilities and other commitments should also be considered. Balancing personal life with a professional artistic career can be challenging. Is your better half on board with your plans, or are you butting heads on the idea? Take it from me: a supportive partner makes all the difference. Once you have evaluated your skills, set goals, and considered personal circumstances, it's time to start strategizing. Are you going all in right away, creating a side hustle, or going through some form of transitional period? This process can be daunting, but having an action plan in place will help you navigate the challenges that may arise. As you noted from my story, I started a side hustle and then started a transitional period once I had made up my mind to go all the way. Basically, I put myself on probation, and when I could see that I had a shot, I went for it. Could you create a detailed plan outlining steps such as building an online presence through a website or social media platforms, researching galleries or alternative platforms for showcasing and selling your art, and networking with other artists or professionals in the industry? Breaking down these tasks into manageable actions will make the transition feel more achievable. It sounds like a big task, but take a few days and make notes. This brainstorming process helps to build a vision of where you will be going. Remember that this decision is unique for each artist; there is no one-size-fits-all answer. Take the time needed for self-reflection and consider all factors carefully before making this significant choice regarding your artistic journey.

Leaving a Lucrative Career?

Transitioning from a stable career into the vibrant and ever-evolving art world can be a thrilling journey of self-discovery. With careful planning and a strategic approach, it is possible to navigate this transition successfully. In this chapter, we will explore some key steps that can help you make this transition as smooth as possible, while also opening up new avenues for personal growth and fulfillment. One important consideration when transitioning into art is avoiding an abrupt career change. Instead, opt for a gradual transition that allows you to ease into your new career while still maintaining stability. Begin by dedicating a few hours each week to your art practice. As your confidence grows and the demand for your work increases, gradually increase the time you dedicate to your art until it becomes your primary focus. Building a solid portfolio is essential when transitioning into the art world. Your portfolio visually represents your skills and talent, showcasing your best work to potential buyers or galleries. Please take the time to create a collection of pieces that show your unique style and artistic vision. I always suggest about twenty paintings if you are a painter. If you sculpt bronzes then this will be much less. Do what makes sense to your situation, but a selection of some sort will give you more exposure to more potential collectors. Include works that demonstrate technical proficiency and emotional depth, allowing viewers to connect with your creations on multiple levels. Networking is crucial in any industry; the art world is no exception. Connect with other artists and art professionals who can offer valuable insights and guidance based on their experiences. Attend local art events such as gallery openings or exhibitions where you can meet like-minded individuals who share your passion for creativity. Engaging in conversations with these individuals not only expands your knowledge but also opens doors for potential collaborations or opportunities in the future. We learn from those who have walked the path before us. I would need to stress the importance of this step. You will never know everything. Keep learning. Keep exploring and keep yourself open to making contacts. I am an introvert. However, I have trained myself over the years to start conversations with people in the art world. Here is a tip: ask the person about themselves. People are happy to talk about themselves. A specific but polite inquiry about their work, establishment, or whatever is relevant, will open a friendly conversation. Please don't barge in with an armful of your paintings and demand attention. You will get nowhere this way.

Remain positive in your conversations. I know it is easy to get down about the economy, politics, and people in general. I heard a wise piece of advice long ago: People may not remember what you said, but they will remember how you made them feel. If you bring a note of positivity and energy into a conversation you will make a good impression. You will be top of mind when an opportunity crops up. Keep this idea in mind during online communications, too, including social media posts and comments. Also, consider joining artist associations or societies. These organizations may provide resources such as workshops, mentorship programs, and networking events. Take advantage of these opportunities to learn from seasoned professionals, gain new perspectives, and establish meaningful connections within the art community. As you navigate this transition, remember that patience and perseverance are not just important, they are your allies. Building a successful career in the arts takes time, dedication, and a willingness to continuously learn and grow. Embrace challenges as opportunities for growth rather than setbacks, and remain open to feedback from both peers and mentors who can provide valuable insights into your artistic development. Trust in your journey and the process, and you will see the fruits of your labor. Finally, it is important to maintain a realistic perspective throughout this process. While pursuing your passion for art is undoubtedly fulfilling, it is crucial to be aware of the financial realities that come with it. Understand that income may not be consistent or predictable initially, especially as you establish yourself in the industry. However, with a well-thought-out financial plan that allows for potential fluctuations in income while still meeting your basic needs, you can navigate these challenges with confidence and peace of mind. Transitioning from another career into art requires careful planning and strategic decision-making. You can pave the way for a successful transition by gradually immersing yourself in your art practice while building a solid portfolio and networking with others in the field. Remember to embrace challenges as opportunities for growth and remain patient as you embark on this exciting new chapter of your life.

The Middle Road Option: The Side Hustle

Yes, there is a middle path that allows artists to enjoy both the security of a traditional job and the benefits of selling their art. This approach involves treating art as a side hustle, where you can dip your toes into the art business without fully committing to it as your primary source of income. Here's how to navigate this middle path effectively:

1. Set Clear Goals and Expectations

Personal and Financial Goals: Decide what you want to achieve with your art side hustle. This could be making extra cash, gaining exposure, or simply enjoying the process of selling your work.

Realistic Expectations: Understanding that a side hustle takes time and effort. Set realistic goals for income and growth.

2. Create a Manageable Art Inventory.

Small, sellable pieces are the way to go. Create a stock of 10-20 small, affordable artworks. These pieces are easier to sell and can attract a wider audience. They are quicker to paint and maybe more flattering than large works that leave you exhausted halfway through because you do not have weeks to work on them.

Consistent Output: Set a schedule to create new pieces regularly without overwhelming yourself. Aim for one or two pieces per month. Then, you may progress to one per weekend. Later, you can complete two per weekend. That is eight works a month. Granted, not every painting may be to your liking. The result, though, will be that within, say, three months, you could have a decent stock level for your first weekend market.

3. Develop a Simple Sales Strategy

Website and Social Media: Set up a simple website with an online store to showcase and sell your work. You do not need an expensive premium shop platform, either. It is more important to showcase your work with good photographs. Buyers can contact you via a simple embedded form on your website. Many buyers prefer this approach to build trust with you before committing to selling.

You will need to set up a payment platform. Options include PayPal. Stripe, Apple Pay, Google Pay, and many more. A simple bank deposit option for local sales can also be concluded.

Use social media to promote your art and connect with potential buyers.

Etsy and Other Platforms: Consider using platforms like Etsy, Saatchi Art, or Redbubble to reach a broader audience. These options keep growing and changing, so do a little research online to see where the hot platforms for selling your art are. Remember that set-it-and-forget-it is not an option if you want regular sales. Just so you know, you will need to send people to your listing. Social media can help with that.

Weekend Markets: Participate in local weekend markets, craft fairs, or car-boot sales. This allows you to interact with potential buyers and get immediate feedback.

Art Fairs and Pop-Ups: Look for opportunities to exhibit at local art fairs or pop-up shops.

Restaurants and Cafes: These places may be looking for decor and want to help local artists. Ask, and you may find yourself a ready and willing venue for your art. Hotel lobbies are another potential marketing spot. A commission on sales could be as low as ten percent.

Bed and Breakfasts and Local Hotels: These places may need a lot of paintings for decor. Ask, and you may get a bundle of sales.

4. Implement Passive Income Streams

Prints and Merchandise: Offer prints of your popular artworks. This allows you to sell multiple copies of a single piece without additional effort. Explore creating merchandise like greeting cards, t-shirts, or mugs featuring your artwork. Online stores can help you do this for free. Fine Art America, Spring and several other print-on-demand platforms can help. Personally, I have not put much effort into these options, but I know artists who get a monthly income this way.

5. Optimize Your Time Management

Dedicated Time Blocks: Allocate specific times during the week for your art side hustle. Balance this with your day job and personal life to avoid burnout. Take your time and enjoy the process. These options discussed in this chapter may take years to test out. If you keep your eye on the number one issue- improving your painting- you will be okay.

Efficient Processes: Streamline your creation and sales processes to maximize productivity. Use tools like templates for marketing materials and automation for social media posts.

6. Test the Waters and Adapt

Track Sales and Feedback: Monitor what sells and what doesn't. Listen to customer feedback and adjust your offerings accordingly. This is why I love weekend markets, pop-ups, and car-boot sales. You get to talk to people and see what they respond to. This is priceless marketing research. It also builds your confidence and your artist's "patter," your ability to talk about your art.

Adapt Your Strategy: Be flexible and willing to change your approach based on your learning. This could mean exploring new sales channels or adjusting your pricing.

7. Plan for Growth or Maintain Stability

Expand Gradually: If your art side hustle gains traction, gradually increase your production and marketing efforts. Consider investing more time and resources as your sales grow.

Full-Time Transition: When your side hustle income begins to match or exceed your day job income, consider whether transitioning to a full-time art career makes sense for you.

Contentment with the Side Hustle

There's no pressure to scale up if the side hustle remains small but enjoyable. Continue creating and selling art at a pace that suits you.

Balance and Satisfaction: Maintain a balance that allows you to enjoy your art without the stress of relying on it for your primary income.

The middle path of treating art as a side hustle offers a flexible and risk-averse way to explore the art market. By creating a manageable inventory, developing a simple sales strategy, and optimizing your time, you can make extra income and enjoy selling your art. This approach allows you to test the waters and adapt without giving up the security of your day job. Whether you grow your side hustle into a full-time career or keep it as a fulfilling hobby, you can find a balance that works for you.

Evaluating Your Skills

As an artist, it is essential to have a clear understanding of your skills and abilities. Evaluating your artistic skills helps you determine your strengths and weaknesses and provides a foundation for growth and improvement. We have discussed this topic briefly in previous chapters, but let us now discuss it in more detail.

Technical Abilities: The first aspect to consider when evaluating your skills is your technical abilities. Do you possess the technical skills required for the medium or style you work? Whether it's painting, sculpting, or digital art, having a solid foundation in technique is crucial. Take some time to assess the quality of your brushstrokes, line work, color, or any other technical elements specific to your chosen medium. If you find areas where you lack proficiency, don't be discouraged. Improvement in technical abilities comes with practice and dedication. Consider taking classes or workshops focused on honing these specific skills. Seeking guidance from experienced artists can provide valuable insights into refining techniques and learning new approaches. Finding a mentor whom you can consult could be the helping hand you need. There are art mentors online or perhaps in your town. Ask around or do an online search. If you admire any particular artist, then ask them. Maybe you have networked another artist at one of those art shows you attended. Be open and ask for a bit of mentoring or critiques on your work. Of course, you must be prepared to pay for such a service. Creativity: Another important factor in evaluating your artistic skills is creativity. How innovative are your ideas? Do you have a unique perspective that sets you apart from others? Creativity is what breathes life into art and captivates viewers' attention. Take some time to reflect on whether your work reflects originality and inventiveness. Are you experimenting with different concepts or pushing boundaries within your chosen style? Don't hesitate to explore new techniques or incorporate unconventional materials into your art practice. This does not mean you have to come up with something utterly new in the history of art. There is little that has not already been done in some form. Instead, make that subtle adaptation to your work. It could be the colors, the brushwork or how you compose the subject.

Indeed the subject itself could distinguish you. Feedback: Beyond specific mentors seeking feedback from trusted sources is an integral part of evaluating one's artistic skills. Reach out to fellow artists who can provide constructive criticism and offer fresh perspectives on your work. Join local art communities or online forums where artists gather to exchange ideas and critique each other's artwork. Remember that feedback should be seen as an opportunity for growth rather than a personal attack. Be open to suggestions and willing to learn from others. Constructive feedback can help you identify areas for improvement and guide your artistic development.

Unique Style: Developing a unique style is an ongoing process that requires self-reflection and experimentation. What I know is that beginners fret over whether they have the right style. I always say that style evolves like your personal signature. Your style defines who you are as an artist at that point in time. In another five years, your style has evolved further. Instead of worrying about style rather focus on your technical issues. Also, make sure that your subject resonates with you. If you love your subject and derive meaning from your work your style will develop along with your growing confidence. Take a look at what elements make your art stand out from others within your chosen medium or genre. Is it the use of color, composition, subject matter, or a combination of these factors? Embrace your individuality and continue to refine your style through practice and exploration.

Continuous Improvement: Evaluating your skills should not be seen as a one-time task but rather as an ongoing process throughout your artistic journey. As you grow as an artist, periodically reassessing your skills will help you identify areas where further development is needed. Attend workshops, courses, or events that focus on expanding artistic skills to stay curious and hungry for knowledge. Collaborate with other artists to gain new perspectives and learn from their experiences. Stay updated with current trends in the art world to ensure that your work remains relevant. Subscribing to a few magazines, for example, can be helpful. By understanding where you stand in terms of skill level and personal growth opportunities, you can make informed decisions about pursuing art as a profession or keeping it as a hobby. Remember that growth is an ongoing process – embrace it wholeheartedly on this beautiful artistic journey.

Setting Artistic Goals

Setting clear and achievable goals is essential for aspiring artists, who must decide whether to sell their work or keep it as a hobby. This chapter will explore the importance of defining their artistic aspirations and establishing targets to guide their creative journey. Artistic goals serve as a roadmap, allowing you to focus on specific milestones and track your progress. Setting both short-term and long-term goals ensures that each step you take aligns with your overall vision for your art. You may be the type of person who finds setting goals easy. You have a Filofax and can plot out tactics, events, and tasks with ease. I admire you. Sadly I am not too hot at this important task. Still, I do my best to pan at least a few weeks ahead. I do try to visualize where I want to be in the next year. This is usually for something specific. Let us set a target for painting sales in November, which is six months away, so I must get twenty works ready for that.

Perhaps it is to complete a course on watercolor painting. Set a date and plot out the small steps to achieve that goal. To begin, could you take some time to reflect on what you hope to achieve with your artistic pursuits? Are you looking to showcase your work in galleries? Do you dream of earning a living solely through art sales? Or perhaps you simply want to improve your skills and share your creations with a broader audience. Once you have identified your main aspirations, break them into smaller, manageable objectives. For example, if one of your long-term goals is to have a solo exhibition in a renowned gallery, could you consider what steps must be taken along the way? This may include building your portfolio, networking with curators and gallery owners, or participating in group exhibitions to gain exposure. It's crucial to establish goals related to external achievements and those centered around personal growth as an artist. Consider what areas of your practice could benefit from improvement or exploration. This could involve experimenting with different mediums or styles, expanding your subject matter repertoire, or honing specific technical skills such as composition or color theory. Remember that setting realistic targets is key. While it's important to dream big and push yourself outside of your comfort zone, be mindful of creating goals that are attainable within the given timeframe. Unrealistically high expectations can lead to frustration and discourage progress. Additionally, consider incorporating measurable elements into each goal whenever possible. For instance, instead of aiming to "improve my painting skills," establish a measurable target such as "complete ten small-scale paintings focusing on capturing light and shadow in the next six months." This way, you will have a clear benchmark to evaluate your progress. Establishing a timeline for each goal is also beneficial. By assigning specific deadlines, you create a sense of urgency and accountability. However, be flexible enough to adapt your timeline if necessary. Artistic growth is often nonlinear, and unexpected opportunities or challenges may arise that require adjustments to your plans. Once you have defined your artistic goals, document them in a visual or written format. Some artists find it helpful to create vision boards or journals where they can regularly revisit their goals and track progress visually. Others prefer written lists or digital tools for easy updating and organization. Remember, these goals are not set in stone. As you evolve as an artist, your aspirations may change or expand. Review and reassess your goals to ensure they align with your artistic vision. As you reflect on setting realistic artistic targets that align with external achievements and personal growth, remember that the journey is as important as the destination.

Assessing Personal Circumstances

In the previous chapters, we explored the importance of evaluating your skills and setting artistic goals. These steps are not just about transitioning from art as a hobby to a professional pursuit, but also about personal growth and fulfillment. Now, let's delve into an equally crucial aspect - your personal circumstances. Your circumstances are not just determining factors for selling your art or keeping it as a hobby, but also opportunities for self-discovery and development. Let's explore the various factors that should be taken into account before making a decision, and how they can contribute to your artistic journey. First and foremost, let us consider financial stability. Selling art can be a rewarding endeavor both creatively and financially, but it is essential to have realistic expectations. Assess your current financial situation and determine if you can invest in art supplies, marketing efforts, and potentially even renting or owning a studio space. Additionally, consider if you are willing to take on the risks associated with fluctuating income as an artist. Selling artwork can sometimes be unpredictable in terms of sales volume and timing. Having a backup plan or financial stability elsewhere is important while building your career as an artist. Another factor worth considering is the time commitment required to sell art professionally. Creating artwork takes time and dedication; however, selling art can demand even more of your time. As an artist pursuing sales opportunities, you will need to allocate time for marketing efforts such as promoting your work online, attending exhibitions or gallery openings, and engaging with potential buyers or clients on social media platforms or networking events. Reflect on whether you can commit the necessary hours outside of creating the artwork itself. Personal obligations also need careful consideration when deciding whether to sell your art or keep it as a hobby. Do you have family responsibilities that may limit the time available to pursue art professionally? Will turning your passion into a profession conflict with other aspects of your life? Understanding how selling artwork may impact your personal life is crucial in making this decision. You need to talk about these issues with your partner to ensure that you both know what you are in for. Reflect upon how comfortable you are with the potential exposure and vulnerability that comes with selling your art. Selling artwork means putting your creations out into the world for public scrutiny and critique. Would you be ready to handle criticism and rejection? It is essential to have a strong sense of self-belief and resilience to navigate the challenges that may come along the way. Lastly, consider the resources and support available to you. Whether it's a network of fellow artists, mentors, or friends who understand and appreciate your artistic journey, or educational resources and platforms like this one, you are not alone in this journey. Surrounding yourself with individuals who share your passion and having access to valuable resources can provide not just encouragement and guidance, but also a sense of security and confidence in your decision-making process. Ultimately, the power to assess your personal circumstances comprehensively and make an informed decision about whether to sell your art or keep it as a hobby lies with you. This process is not just about considering financial stability, time commitment, personal obligations, comfort with exposure and vulnerability, and the presence of a support system. It's about taking charge of your artistic journey, understanding your own needs and aspirations, and making a decision that aligns with your unique circumstances and goals. Assessing personal circumstances is integral to deciding whether to pursue art professionally or keep it as a hobby. Now that we have covered this and many other tips on evaluating your decision, let's move forward and take the big leap into your new art business.

Making the Transition

The time has come to transition from art as a hobby to pursue it professionally. Transitioning from hobbyist to professional artist requires careful thought and preparation. It is important to approach this transition with determination and a clear vision of what you hope to achieve.

I want to tell you about my first year as a full-time artist. This story may contain a few nuggets of information. In the coming chapters, we will discuss more tactics, strategies, and tips for your business success.

Once you decide to transition from part-time to full-time artist, or maybe you're going straight into a full-time artist from your day job, you really have to focus and go for it with determination. Every person is going to have a different approach, perhaps, and a different emphasis on what they want to do with their new life. For me, it was a case of exiting one business in one year and then starting a new business in the new year. There was not too much time for holiday. None in fact.

Part of that transition period involved moving house as well, so there was a lot of that complication. Perhaps in your case, you won't be moving house, but you will be setting up your studio and getting it efficient. Painting out a new studio to make it look fresh and clean for art students. That alone takes a lot of work.

In my situation, I had various ideas I wanted to go ahead with immediately. First of all was physical workshops. So I put together a painting workshop based on a two-day workshop, and I would focus on what I'm teaching now in my Painterly Workshop online and in my coaching classes.

My studio had enough space for about six to eight students during the two-day workshop. So, I had to consider making the space comfortable enough as it was. It was a squeeze to fit eight people, but still, it was done.

That meant getting things like easels that everybody could work from, chairs so people could sit, and a studio that also helped me give lectures. So I set up a flat-screen TV on the wall and attached that to a laptop, and I could do a slide presentation, as it were, and show examples of what I wanted to teach in the class. Then there would be demonstrations, and then students would get stuck into a series of paintings, and I would help each person.

If you've been in an art workshop, this is probably similar to what you've experienced before. There would be breaks as well. Breaks for tea and breaks for lunch. My wife was helping out by providing snacks and tea-time treats.

It was quite an intensive two days. I had a great response. Students came from all over the country and there were even repeat attendances. That was very gratifying and encouraging.

I enjoyed the workshops. I have to say they were learning experiences, not only for the art students but also for me. I learned how to present, how to speak clearly and effectively so that people would understand the concepts, and how to work with people in an inspirational way. However, after a year of doing workshops, I decided it was too much to fit into a home studio situation.

There was quite a lot of disruption for my family during those workshops. Also, I must say they were exhausting for me. This is not a complaint, but it does mean that you must consider your energy and personality. I am a typical introvert, and with hindsight, I am more suited to working one-on-one with a student. I could also tell that economically, it was difficult for people to get away, pay for accommodation, travel, and everything else that goes into getting away fo workshops.

I then focused more on online teaching, as it appeared that I had students all over the world who wanted to do art lessons with me. Of course, this started very small. But even if you are teaching three or four people from around the world, that is still a lot less stressful than putting on a physical workshop for two days.

The nice part of teaching online is that you can work with people for a few hours and then take a break, recharge, prepare, and so on. As I mentioned before, this was a lot less demanding on me, an introverted artist.

Extroverts. on the other hand, will enjoy large groups and get a lot of energy from that sort of stimulation. Extroverts can also do online classes, but it may be secondary as they miss the buzz of working in the busy workshop situation. If you are like that, then you may need to plan on holding workshops around the country. There are many artists who are happy to offer a venue or organize a venue in their town. Art societies and clubs are always looking for guest artists to teach their members. You may find yourself establishing a nice tour schedule you can follow for years. This can lead to international teaching too. How about hosting a workshop for a week in France, Portugal and Tuscany? Many artists do this regularly, and there are organizations that help make the arrangements. Sounds like an option worth looking into if that idea excites you. After all, you get to see the most beautiful places in the world, and most of the costs are paid for. Neat!

So, the transition year focused on physical workshops, which in turn gave way to a focus on online teaching. The important thing to note was that I could make an income teaching from the get-go. Scratch the fear of not being able to survive. In the worst-case scenario, I may have had to dip into the emergency fund. In fact I did that a few times because there were repairs to our new fixer-upper house. Avoid that complication if you can.

In year two, I expanded the online teaching into coaching and included new courses on various topics, from oils to acrylics and gouache. So that was a very busy year, year number two, setting up online courses.

In the gaps between, I started my YouTube channel. I had no great expectations for it. It was simply a way to introduce myself to a wider audience and provide helpful videos.

I could just put the channel out there. I could decide on topics I wanted and put them out there for people to enjoy. In between the online lessons and YouTube, I was writing, contributing to my blog, and working on book ideas for creativity.

All of these things required a learning curve. A learning curve using different applications, a learning curve in research, and, in fact, a learning curve on how to communicate in writing and on camera. None of these things could be done without making embarrassing mistakes and looking a bit foolish. But the only person who suffered from these mistakes was, in fact, myself, and I was dealing with my issues about whether I was making a complete idiot of myself or not. Apparently, no one else cared, so there was no real harm done.

So that was the transition year. Everything since then has simply been polishing that strategy, improving it, building on it, getting myself more confident, improving my materials, improving my camera work, improving everything I could, and still delivering an effective and helpful learning experience. Everything was centered on that one aspect, which is giving artists around the world a better learning experience.

In each thing I did, I was trying to improve. I was trying to give people what they wanted instead of trying to figure out what I wanted to do. Ideally, I would figure out what we both wanted: something I could enjoy doing and something that was actually helpful to other artists around the world. The other issue with transitioning, of course, into this full-time business was trying to generate cash flow. And that was once again a case of multiple streams of income.

There were still my paintings; I was still putting out paintings and trying to sell small paintings to people around the world. Then there were the online lessons, from free to small paid lessons and then larger courses that paid a bit more. And then there were the books.

The books were not really a financial strategy. That's more of a way to start a relationship with somebody that might turn into paid courses down the line. Building these trails and funnels, if you could call them that, although I don't really like that word. Other marketers talk about leaving breadcrumbs for people to discover you and lead them to you, but I don't really like that idea either. The simple fact is, all I wanted to do was provide useful and helpful information, have fun painting, and meet new people. Everyone is different, and nobody can be treated as if they're just a number. That is not the way I like to be treated and I was never going to become a "marketing guru" to get rich. Or pretend to be some rich artist.

I don't have that approach, and hopefully, I never will. I'd rather have a dozen loyal and happy fans than a hundred people who just move on by and I don't connect with. Also, in this first year, I kept trying to study as much as I could. I read up about online marketing, read about art topics as well, got to know my topics like impressionism, and learned more about techniques and applying them.

You never know everything, and as long as you can provide something new and useful, you are helping. It sounds like a lot, and I suppose it was, but I also found time to try to have some fun—not just painting, but getting out, walking on the beach, and enjoying the new experience.

When I started working full-time as an artist, I thought I would be under severe stress about replicating my past business and making an income. Instead, I discovered that none of that really mattered. I was doing what I enjoyed. There was enough money to take care of the necessities, and I didn't have to go into debt.

What more do you need? If you can pull that off, then you are in a very happy situation. As long as you keep working and trying to improve the work you do and be more helpful to other people, you will always have a source of income, enjoyment, and, most importantly, purpose. You must have a purpose for getting up each day and doing what you do. The purpose is not to make money.

The purpose is to help other people; if you can, you will never be without a living. You will make your living and feel fulfilled.

It's simply about making a respectable and decent living that will take care of you and your loved ones. That is all one needs.

I tried to apply the lessons I've spoken about in previous chapters and constantly see where I could improve with little steps, step by step, little tweaks, little things. It's not about getting everything right in year one, and then you can just sit back and cruise. It's making a start and gradually improving as you go. We can go into a few more tactics and strategies in greater detail as we go through the rest of the book.

But just so you know, once you make that step over the line into the new life, you'll find all the fears melt away. Now you're busy doing what you love, and it's so much simpler than you thought it was going to be. Just stick to your plan, keep working at it, keep improving, and keep scaling up little by little. Work with integrity and be helpful.

Marketing Your Work

Now that you have decided to sell your art and pursue it professionally, it is crucial to understand how to market your work effectively. This chapter will explore various strategies for marketing your art on different platforms, such as galleries, online marketplaces, social media platforms, and networking events. Galleries: One traditional avenue for artists to showcase and sell their work is through galleries. Galleries provide a physical space where art enthusiasts can appreciate and purchase artwork. When approaching galleries, research is key. Look for galleries that align with your artistic style and target audience. Visit their exhibitions and familiarize yourself with their curatorial choices. When approaching a gallery for representation, prepare a portfolio showcasing your best works. Include an artist statement that captures your vision and motivations behind your creations. Most galleries typically require an application along with high-quality photographs of your artwork. Online Marketplaces: With the rise of technology, online marketplaces have become increasingly popular for artists seeking wider exposure and potential customers worldwide. Platforms like Etsy or Saatchi Art provide accessible spaces to showcase and sell your creations. Creating an appealing online presence is vital when utilizing these platforms. High-quality photographs of your artwork are essential in capturing the essence of each piece. Write detailed descriptions that engage potential buyers by sharing the inspiration behind each creation or any unique techniques utilized. Social Media Platforms: Social media has revolutionized how artists connect with their audience globally. Platforms like Instagram have become virtual galleries where artists can share their work directly with followers who appreciate their style. To effectively market your art on social media platforms: 1) Consistency: Regularly post new artwork, works in progress, and behind-the-scenes glimpses into your creative process. This consistency helps build anticipation and engagement with your audience. 2) Engage with Your Audience: Respond promptly to comments, messages, and inquiries. Engaging with your followers fosters a sense of connection and builds trust. 3) Hashtags: Utilize relevant hashtags to increase the visibility of your posts. Research popular hashtags within the art community while also incorporating niche-specific tags that align with your style or subject matter.

Do not buy followers. There are services that offer to multiply your followers "organically" and above board. It is a scam. You will get fake, non-engaged followers, and your account may be suspended. You can save your money for your actual business, not scam services. 4) Collaborations: Seek opportunities to collaborate with other artists or influencers within the art community. These collaborations can expose your work to new audiences and foster cross-promotion. This may seem unlikely when you are starting, but actually, it does start to happen with time. Many offers are not worth taking up. For example, I will get offers from a company that wants to add a blog article to my website. They promise that the article aligns with my audience. What is the article about? Oh, a teeth whitening product? Okay bye! However, collaborating with another artist could include doing alternate podcast interviews, a painting demonstration for our respective YouTube channels, or a review of art materials. I see no harm as long as these are done honestly and with full disclosure. The guiding principle for me is whether this opportunity will be helpful to my audience. Typically, there is no money exchanged either. These collaborations are purely for exposure to a new audience or exciting content. Networking Events: Attending networking events such as art fairs, exhibitions, and workshops is an excellent way to connect with fellow artists, collectors, gallery owners, and potential buyers. Networking allows you to showcase your work in person while building relationships within the art industry. These events formed a big part of my early exposure to art buyers. It is a great way to meet collectors and build relationships with potentially lifelong fans. When attending these events: 1) Prepare Your Elevator Pitch: Be able to succinctly explain who you are as an artist and what sets you apart from others. This will help you confidently present yourself when conversing about your artwork. 2) Business Cards: Have professional business cards with essential contact information such as your name, website/portfolio link, email address, and social media handles. These cards are a tangible reminder of who you are as an artist when someone expresses interest in your work. These cards are still better than any digital business card app. 3) Follow-up: After networking events, follow up with those you connected with by sending personalized emails expressing gratitude for their time or discussing potential collaborations or sales opportunities.

More on this in the next chapter. Please keep one thing in mind. You can learn much about marketing and engaging with people from books on this topic. From books for artists like this one to general marketing books and motivational authors like Brian Tracey and Napoleon Hill. Study like your career depends on it, because it does.

Conclusion: Marketing plays a crucial role in successfully selling your artwork. Whether through traditional avenues like galleries or online platforms such as social media or online marketplaces, it is essential to create a strong online presence that showcases the unique qualities of your artwork. Remember to engage with followers regularly on social media platforms and take advantage of networking events to build connections within the art community. By effectively marketing your work, you increase your chances of reaching a broader audience and achieving success in your artistic journey. In the next chapter, we will explore the importance of continuous improvement in your artistic journey and ways to enhance your skills through workshops, courses, collaborations with other artists, and staying up-to-date with current trends in the art world.

More Ways to Show Your Work

Showcasing your art effectively can significantly enhance your reputation, credibility, and income. Here are key strategies to consider:

1. Entering Art Competitions to Build a Reputation

Exposure: Participating in art competitions can provide significant exposure. Being featured or winning awards enhances your visibility and validates your skills.

Marketing Opportunities: Competition achievements can be used in marketing materials. Mentioning awards in your biography, website, and social media profiles helps build credibility. Go about this tastefully. Overwhelming your social media feed with self-congratulatory posts can be self-defeating, but you are not that sort of person.

Networking: Competitions often provide networking opportunities with other artists, gallery owners, and potential buyers. If you have these events in your locality then go for it. Sign up, do your best, have fun, and soak up as much from the experience as you can.

2. Taking on Commissions

I discussed this briefly in Chapter 3. Commissions can be a steady and lucrative source of income. Consider a portrait artist, muralist, or photographer. These artists can survive solely on commissions. Clients pay for bespoke pieces, providing financial stability. Advertising your services is vital to reaching new clients. In many ways, marketing is similar for any artist, but drawing attention to your availability to take on commissions must always be stressed. More marketing ideas will be discussed later in this book.

Client Satisfaction: While satisfying client preferences, try to maintain a balance between client demands and your artistic integrity. Clear communication about the creative process can help manage expectations. Put everything in writing so that you are all on the same page. Get a deposit of ten percent minimum upfront on acceptance of the commission to cover your initial costs. The deposit could be more depending on the nature of the project.

Flexibility and Integrity: Be willing to compromise to some extent but ensure the final work still reflects your style and vision. This maintains your authenticity as an artist.

3. Strategic Pricing

Increase your prices regularly to keep up with inflation and rising material costs. This ensures your practice remains sustainable.

Signal of Quality: Higher prices can signal quality and exclusivity. Positioning your work in a higher price bracket can attract serious collectors and buyers. There are other schools of thought on this contentious topic. I know artists who charge huge sums for work that is no different from the work of artists who charge a fraction of that price. The high-priced artist is positioning himself for a particular type of client. Positioning is a marketing tactic. Can you sustain this if sales are harder to come by when times are tough? Some say that the rich stay rich no matter what.

On the other hand, pricing for the middle-income bracket may increase sales or keep sales more consistent. Do you feel happier pricing at this level? This may be due to confidence issues. You need to assess your strategy. Discuss this with trusted artists or a gallerist.

Another option is having different types of work to cover different markets. Your smaller studies at more affordable prices. Prints or other merchandise. Then, your larger or more resolved works for higher-income individuals or corporate clients. Consider a "masterworks" line of art that you charge much more. There are ways to position yourself. You have to think and try things all the time.

Consistency: To maintain credibility, ensure your pricing strategy is consistent across different sales platforms and venues. Once you set your pricing, make sure you are consistent. You do not want similar work selling for a bargain elsewhere because this will upset your bigger client, who may feel cheated.

4. Diverse Sales Channels

Galleries offer professional representation, helping to reach high-end buyers and collectors. Gallery representation often includes invitations to exhibitions and events, increasing your network and exposure.

Art Fairs and Shows allow you to interact directly with buyers, receive feedback, and build personal connections. These events attract a large audience, providing significant exposure and potential sales opportunities. On the other hand, these events can sometimes flop, and you can find them to be a huge waste of time and money. Do your research first. Go to shows and markets that have a proven success record for attracting solid crowd attendance.

Online Platforms like Etsy and Facebook Marketplace offer accessible ways to sell your art to a global audience. Personally, I cannot confirm this because I do not use these platforms. However, there are very successful artists using them. YouTube research is particularly useful as you can watch videos made by artists with a proven track record sharing their wisdom on these platforms.

Early in my online marketing, I decided to build my platform. Social media would be a way of attracting people back to my platform to get more from me. Although this may take me out of a huge market, I do feel that I own my own platform. These other social media platforms or communal marketplaces can change on a dime. It is like being a tenant, with much less security.

Actively promote your listings through social media, newsletters, and other online marketing strategies to drive traffic and sales.

5. Consistent, Long-Term Marketing and Advertising

Instead of spreading yourself thin, focus on one or two key marketing channels. Whether it's social media, email newsletters, or blog content, consistent effort in selected areas yields better results.

Content Creation: Regularly create engaging content that showcases your process, finished works, and behind-the-scenes glimpses. This keeps your audience engaged and interested. I wrote a book called The Art of Content

Marketing in its second edition. There is much there on the topic of creating content.

Content creation includes writing blogs, making videos, writing books, creating posts on social media, creating guides, and many other ways to produce something that intends to communicate a message to someone else. In our case, it will build your credibility and attract followers, new clients, leads, or subscribers. However, content creation is not for everyone. Some loathe the time and thought that must go into it. It's better not to bother than start and give up, leaving you feeling depressed and unmotivated. However, if you love your topic and communication method, you will go far by sticking to that method. For example, if you love creating videos for YouTube. Make that your number one focus. All other content you create will be to lead people to your YouTube channel.

Which is Better, Galleries or Art Shows?

Participation in local and international art shows increases your visibility and helps build a reputation within the art community.

Participating in art shows and traditional galleries both have their benefits for showcasing your artwork:

Art shows allow you to interact directly with potential customers, practice your sales pitch, and learn what resonates with buyers. Conversations with interested buyers at shows can lead to commission opportunities where you create custom pieces for them. In addition to originals, you can offer more affordable prints and merchandise at shows to appeal to a broader audience. Art shows allow you to reach customers who may not frequent traditional galleries. It is not just your work that you promote but also any teaching you may do.

Traditional Galleries: Being represented by a respected gallery lends credibility and prestige to your work. Galleries have established relationships with art collectors and can introduce your work to potential buyers. Gallery representation allows you to price your work at the higher end of the market. Galleries provide a steady stream of sales opportunities through their exhibitions and events.

This all presumes that the gallery is doing all these proactive things. Very often, a gallery does nothing more than open its doors at 10 a.m. and close them again at 16h30. This type of gallery is not going to grow your sales. They will depress you, and you will collect your work from them, knowing you can do much better as your salesperson. If you have a proactive gallery supporting you, do your best to support their efforts. Be available to help market your work at events, meet potential buyers, and keep in regular touch with your gallery, sending them new work as required.

The best approach often involves a combination of art shows and gallery representation to maximize exposure and sales. Participating in shows can help you build your skills and audience, while gallery representation provides access to collectors and higher price points. Ultimately, the right path depends on your specific goals and the type of work you create.

Showcasing your art effectively involves a combination of strategic actions, from entering competitions and taking on commissions to setting the right prices and diversifying sales channels. Consistent, focused marketing and advertising efforts are crucial in building long-term awareness and interest in your work. By leveraging these strategies, you can enhance your reputation, reach a broader audience, and create a sustainable income stream from your art. Remember to maintain a balance between meeting market demands and staying true to your artistic vision.

How to Market Your Non-Traditional Art?

Nontraditional art refers to artwork that does not neatly fit into conventional art categories or styles. It often incorporates unconventional materials, techniques, or approaches that challenge traditional boundaries.

Some key characteristics of non-traditional art include:

Hybrid techniques: Combining digital and manual processes, such as manipulating digital photographs and then printing and hand-painting the results.

Experimental media: Using unexpected materials like glass, metal, or wood as substrates for artwork.

Abstract or pop-art styles: Leaning toward more modern, abstract, or pop-art aesthetics that may not align with traditional representational art.

Pushing boundaries: Embracing innovative approaches that expand the definition of art.

While non-traditional art may not always fit comfortably into established categories, there are opportunities to successfully showcase this type of work. Strategies include:

Targeting galleries open to experimentation: Seeking out galleries willing to push the limits and showcase unique, boundary-pushing art.

Participating in art shows: Attending art fairs and craft shows can expose you to new audiences and provide opportunities for direct sales.

Building a strong portfolio: Having a large, consistent body of work demonstrates to galleries that an artist is serious and committed.

Ultimately, the key to success with nontraditional art is finding the right venues and audiences that appreciate the work's unique qualities and vision. You can help this process with the following ideas:

1. Highlight Your Unique Selling Points

Emphasize what sets your work apart: Highlight the unique aspects of your hybrid digital photography and manual manipulation techniques to differentiate your work from traditional photography and art categories.

Showcase your inventory: Galleries love artists with a large body of work and consistent production, so ensure you have a diverse and extensive inventory to display.

Use the "money wall" principle: Display high-priced items alongside lower-priced ones to create a sense of value and make your work more appealing to galleries.

3. Prepare a Strong Marketing Strategy: Gather testimonials and stories from collectors and stories about their responses to your work to demonstrate its appeal.

Share any success you have had in direct sales or other marketing efforts to demonstrate your potential for success in a gallery setting.

Use social media and online platforms to promote your work on platforms like Facebook and Etsy to drive traffic to your online store and increase visibility.

4. Believe in Yourself and Your Work. Confidence is key. Believe in your unique style and its value to the art world. This confidence will shine through in your marketing and interactions with galleries. Be open to feedback and willing to adjust your approach as needed to better suit the needs of galleries and collectors.

By following these steps, you can effectively pitch your nontraditional artwork to galleries and increase your chances of success in the art market.

Marketing for Commissions

Advertising for commission work is crucial for artists looking to expand their client base and generate steady income. Despite the risk of meeting "difficult clients," this risk can be minimized with common sense approaches. Never be desperate. If done correctly, commission-based art practices can be lucrative and fulfilling. Here are several effective ways and places for artists to advertise their commission work:

Online Platforms

1. Personal Website: Create a dedicated page for commission work, showcasing previous commissions, outlining the process, and providing clear contact information. Write blog posts about your commission process, client tips, and case studies of past projects. People searching for commission artists online will more likely discover you as you have content dealing with commissions.

2. Social Media

Instagram: Post regularly about your commission process, share finished commissions, and use relevant hashtags. Respond to comments and direct messages to engage with followers. Keep an eye out for scam offers, though. There are many offers to sell your art as an NFT, for instance. Also, if you use Instagram, set up two-factor authentication in your settings to make it more difficult for your account to be hacked. Not to sound negative, as I use Instagram, but many scammers are out there.

Facebook: Use your artist page to promote commissions, share client testimonials, and join art-related groups to network and advertise your services.

Pinterest: Create boards showcasing your commission work, process, and testimonials. Link pins back to your website for more details.

3. Online Marketplaces

Etsy: Set up a shop offering custom artwork. Clearly define your commission process, pricing, and examples of past work.

Fiverr and Upwork: Offer your commission services on these freelancing platforms if your work fits this avenue. Create detailed gig descriptions with examples of your work.

4. Art-Specific Platforms

DeviantArt: Use DeviantArt to showcase your portfolio and offer commission services. Participate in community forums and groups to promote your work.

ArtStation: Post your commission work and process, and join groups or forums related to your style or medium.

Redbubble and Society6: While primarily print-on-demand platforms, they offer exposure to potential clients who might be interested in commissions.

Local Opportunities

1. Art Galleries and Local Art Shows

Exhibit Work: Display your work at local galleries and art shows. Include information about commission services on your artist statements and price tags.

Networking: Engage with visitors and other artists, and distribute business cards or flyers detailing your commission services.

2. Community Centers and Libraries

Bulletin Boards: Post flyers or business cards on community bulletin boards.

Workshops and Classes: Teach art classes or workshops and mention your commission services to attendees.

3. Local Businesses

Coffee Shops and Restaurants: Partner with local businesses to display your art and include information about commission services.

Professional Networks

1. Networking Events and Conferences: Participate in local and regional art fairs and festivals. Have a booth dedicated to showcasing your commission work and process. Join art associations or guilds to network with other artists and potential clients.

2. Referrals and Word of Mouth: Encourage satisfied clients to refer you to friends and family. Offer incentives, such as discounts on future commissions, for successful referrals. If you never ask, you will limit your work opportunities. You do not want to sound desperate and salesy, but you can bring these topics up in a friendly and positive way.

3. Collaborate with other artists, designers, or professionals who can refer clients to you. If you can support each other you may find extra work by having a few more people out there who know what you offer.

Digital Marketing

1. Email Marketing: Newsletter: Create a regular newsletter showcasing new work, available commission slots, and client testimonials. Encourage subscribers to share with their networks.

Personalized Outreach: Send personalized emails to potential clients highlighting your commission services and past work.

You may be wondering how to get potential clients to sign up for your email list. This is a very important step. Could you offer something in return for the favor? Marketers call this a lead magnet. I think of it as a thank-you gift and a mark of good faith. Here are some ideas you can try out:

Five ideas for email lead magnets that artists can use to build their email lists:

1. Free video tutorial or art lesson: This is my favorite because it is a high-value gift.

- Create a short, high-quality video demonstrating a specific art technique or skill

- Offer it as a free download in exchange for signing up for your email list

- Showcase your teaching abilities and provide value to potential subscribers

2. Exclusive behind-the-scenes content

- Give subscribers a sneak peek into your creative process or studio

- Share photos, videos, or stories that are only available to email list members

- Make them feel like insiders and build a stronger connection with your audience

3. Printable coloring pages or sketches

- Design beautiful, intricate coloring pages or sketches featuring your artwork

- Offer them as free downloads for email subscribers

- Appeal to art lovers and those interested in your style

4. Discounts or special offers

- Offer a special discount code or early access to new artwork releases

- Provide value to subscribers and incentivize them to join your list

- Ensure the offer is enticing enough to encourage sign-ups

5. Comprehensive art resource guide

- Create a comprehensive guide covering topics like art supplies, techniques, or art history

- Compile it into a downloadable PDF or eBook

- Position yourself as an expert in your field and provide immense value to subscribers

When creating your lead magnet, focus on providing genuine value. Make it easy to access by requiring only an email address for download. Promote your lead magnet across your website, social media channels, and in-person events to maximize visibility and list growth. This is easy to say but takes some effort to do. Still, it is well worth the effort, as it is your business that we are talking about. A strong email list can be the foundation for a sustainable art business. Take some time to brainstorm a high value offering and start building an email list as soon as possible.

2. Paid Advertising: Social adverts are the reality of social media results. Organic traffic is throttled by cunning algorithms, and the game is rigged in favor of the house. All sorts of similes there, but you get the picture. If you want the views, you need to pay for them. Or do you?

They may say all you need to do is use targeted ads on platforms like Facebook, Instagram, and Pinterest to reach potential clients interested in your art. Run Google Ads targeting keywords related to art commissions and your specific style or medium. Sit back and watch the emails come flooding in.

Crickets!

I used social media ads about ten years ago and Google search ads. They were pretty effective and easy to set up. Nowadays, all I hear is that ads cost too much, are difficult to set up, and results are spotty as people no longer look at ads much when scrolling through social media. I think there is a much better way for artists. We create beautiful things. We have a message to convey through art, words and images. Put that out there and be consistent. Many of the other suggestions here, such as building your email list, will deliver much more than throwing money after adverts.

3. Content Marketing

Blogging and Vlogging: This gets a bit more creative and technically challenging. However, if you are game to learn a few new things, then this stuff can make a big impact. Much of it can be done via good smartphones too. Create content about the commission process, tips for clients, and behind-the-scenes looks at your work. Use platforms like YouTube, Medium, and your blog.

Podcasts and Webinars: There is a lot more commitment to the learning curve here, but it is doable. There are many resources, how-to videos, courses, and books on these topics. Dive into them if you have the curiosity. Participate in or create podcasts and webinars discussing your commission process and experiences.

By leveraging online platforms, local opportunities, professional networks, and digital marketing strategies, you can effectively advertise your commission work and attract a diverse range of clients. Consistent promotion, quality engagement, and showcasing your unique artistic process will help you build a strong reputation and a steady stream of commission requests.

Consistent Improvement

As an artist, your journey of self-discovery and growth never truly ends. Your desire to constantly improve your skills and evolve is what sets you apart from the rest. How do you consistently improve? Here are a few suggestions. **Workshops and courses** are fantastic opportunities to refine your skills and learn new techniques. Seek local art centers, community colleges, or online platforms offering workshops or classes in areas you wish to develop further. Whether mastering a new medium, exploring different painting styles, or honing your drawing abilities, these learning experiences can provide invaluable guidance from experienced instructors and expose you to fresh perspectives. I like to remind myself that if I can learn one new thing from a painting demonstration or studying a Master painting, it has been a successful learning experience. Applying that one thing to my painting can spark a dramatic change in my work. One that will take my painting level higher and bring me greater fulfillment. It will also delight a future collector. Collaborations with other artists can also be a catalyst for growth. Working alongside fellow creatives allows you to exchange ideas and inspires you to push boundaries and step out of your comfort zone. Consider joining art collectives or participating in group exhibitions where collaboration is encouraged. Through these collaborations, you will gain insights into different artistic approaches while fostering connections within the art community. Staying up-to-date with current trends in the art world is important for any artist seeking continuous improvement. Attend gallery openings, art fairs, and exhibitions to stay informed about emerging artists and innovative techniques. Engage in conversations with fellow artists and collectors; their perspectives may inspire new ideas or shed light on upcoming trends. Remember that this does not mean studying the latest abstract art trend if you prefer traditional painting subjects. Every genre of art is developing. As artists emerge, they bring new ideas and fresh perspectives. There may be something new and exciting that helps you see a new path for your art, too. In addition to external influences, don't forget the importance of introspection. Take time for self-reflection. Identify areas where you excel and others where improvement is needed. Keep a sketchbook or journal handy to document thoughts, ideas, and observations that arise during this process. Reviewing these notes can help identify patterns or recurring themes that may guide future exploration. Experimentation is key to evolving as an artist. Don't hesitate to step outside your comfort zone and try new techniques, subjects, or styles. Push the boundaries of your creativity by exploring unfamiliar territories. Allow yourself to make mistakes and learn from them; it is through experimentation that groundbreaking discoveries are often made. While self-improvement is vital, it is equally important to seek feedback from others. Share your work with trusted friends, fellow artists, or mentors who can offer constructive criticism. Their perspectives can provide fresh insights and highlight areas you may have overlooked. Technology has opened up a world of possibilities for artists today. Embrace digital tools that can enhance and streamline your artistic process. Explore digital art software, graphic tablets, or 3D printing if they align with your creative vision. While traditional mediums hold their charm, integrating technology into your practice can open up new avenues for creativity and expand your skill set. This is not that simple for me. One of the things I love about Impressionist oil painting is that I can follow in the footsteps of Masters over a century ago. I am using almost the same paints, and in some cases, the tools are unchanged. Raphael Paris Classic brushes, for example, were used by Monet. We can still use them today. However, I can plan a painting using computer art software, too. Tha is a handy tool to use at times. Keep with the spirit of the creative process and use the tools that make that process more effective. Never underestimate the power of networking in the art world. Attend local art events, join online artist communities, or participate in juried exhibitions to connect with other like-minded individuals. Building relationships within the art community provides support and opens doors to potential collaborations or opportunities for showcasing your work. Remember that growth is a continuous process; there is no final destination for improving as an artist. Embrace every opportunity for learning and growth throughout your creative journey. Stay curious, stay open-minded, and never stop challenging yourself. As you embark on this journey of self-discovery as an artist, remember that it is ultimately your passion and dedication that will drive you forward. Trust in yourself and your abilities. Never lose sight of the joy that creating art brings to your life.

Keep Balanced

As an artist, your journey of growth and development never truly ends. It's not just about thriving in the ever-evolving art world, but also about the personal growth and fulfillment that comes from dedicating time and effort towards continuous improvement. Finding the delicate balance between creation and business is a part of this journey. Feedback and Reflection: Constructive feedback is not just a part of an artist's growth, it's a catalyst. Seek input from peers, mentors, or even your audience to gain fresh perspectives on your work. Embrace criticism as an opportunity for improvement rather than taking it personally. Reflect on this feedback with an open mind and identify areas that could benefit from refinement or experimentation. Self-reflection is equally important in honing your artistic skills. Take time to analyze your work objectively. Ask yourself questions such as: What aspects do I excel at? Where can I make improvements? What are my strengths that I can build upon? By continuously evaluating your artwork, you will be able to set new goals for yourself that align with your artistic vision. Balancing Creation and Business: Artists often find themselves torn between their passion for creating art and managing the business aspect of their craft - selling and marketing their work. It's not about sacrificing one for the other, but about finding a balance that allows you to pursue both without feeling overwhelmed. Allocate specific times for creating art without any distractions or interruptions. This dedicated time allows you to fully immerse yourself in your creative process and explore new ideas. By setting aside regular periods for creation, you ensure that your artistic growth continues. Simultaneously, it is important to allocate time for managing the business side of your art career. This could include updating your portfolio, networking with potential buyers or galleries, and promoting your work on various platforms. Set aside specific weekly hours to focus on these activities, ensuring they do not overshadow the time dedicated to creating art. I have discovered that marketing and business take much more time than painting. If that shocks you, then I am sorry, but you will find that out, too. You may spend two hours painting per day, but expect to spend six hours on business. Balance does not mean fifty-fifty. Fortunately that two hours of painting is sufficient to balance my six hours spent on business. Finding a harmonious balance between creation and business allows you ample opportunity for artistic growth while positioning yourself in the market. Remember that being successful as an artist requires exceptional talent as well as effective promotion and selling strategies. Continuous improvement is an essential aspect of every artist's journey. By dedicating time to ongoing learning, seeking feedback and reflection, and finding the balance between creation and business, you will cultivate an environment of growth and development within your artistic practice. Remember that every step taken towards improvement brings you closer to becoming the best version of yourself as an artist. It is also you who gets to decide what is the best version.

Multiple Streams of Income

In the previous chapters, we have explored the various aspects of selling your art and whether or not you should keep it as a hobby. One thing that has become clear is that relying solely on art sales can be risky. In this chapter, we explore diversifying your income with multiple revenue streams. It is easily my favorite idea for a thriving solo artist. Diversifying your income is crucial for any artist looking to sustain themselves financially in the long run. While selling your artwork may be the primary source of income, it is essential to consider other avenues to supplement and stabilize your finances. One potential stream of income for artists is teaching. Offering workshops, classes, or even online tutorials can provide you with a stable income and allow you to share your expertise and passion with others. Teaching can be a rewarding experience as you get to inspire and guide aspiring artists on their creative journey while earning an additional source of revenue. Another way to diversify your income is through commissioned work tailored to clients' needs. Accepting commissions allows you to create art for individuals or businesses willing to pay for personalized pieces. This provides financial stability and an opportunity for artistic growth as you explore different themes and styles based on client specifications. Merchandising can be an excellent avenue for generating additional income. Creating and selling merchandise featuring your art opens up new possibilities beyond traditional artwork sales. Prints, apparel, and home decor items are just a few examples of products that can feature your unique creations and appeal to a broader audience who may want something more tangible than original artwork. Freelance opportunities in related fields such as graphic design, illustration, or digital art. Many companies constantly seek talented artists who can bring their creative vision to life through various projects. Authors may need an illustrator for their book. You can help out there. Designing a book cover can be extra income for you. Freelancing provides both financial stability and exposure within different industries while allowing you to expand your artistic skills beyond the traditional canvas.

If you are handy with DIY, you could build frames for paintings. That is lucrative work for a part-time source of income. How about custom gilding of frames? By diversifying your income through these various streams, you minimize the financial risks associated with relying solely on art sales and open up new opportunities for growth and creativity. Embracing multiple revenue sources can help you weather any economic downturns or market fluctuations that may affect the demand for your artwork. However, balancing these different income streams and your primary focus as an artist is important. While exploring multiple avenues can be beneficial, ensuring that your artistic integrity remains intact is crucial. Don't let financial considerations overshadow your passion and artistic vision. Diversifying your income as an artist is a smart move to secure financial stability and expand your creative horizons. Teaching, accepting commissions, merchandising, and freelancing are all viable options that can supplement your art sales revenue. Remember to find a balance between these income streams while staying true to yourself as an artist. By embracing multiple revenue sources, you protect yourself financially and nurture a thriving artistic career in the long run. Multiple streams of income can help you navigate the complex world of art business with confidence and make informed decisions about commercializing your creativity. Not to mention giving you a breather when times get tight. That extra income stream is very handy.

The Argument Againtst and For Gallery Representation

When you decide to take your art further, either for extra income in a side hustle or full-time, you may consider gallery representation as the holy grail to be secured at all costs. This idea can fixate in your mind to the extent that you can hardly think of anything else. You may have visions of sold-out exhibitions arranged for you by a benevolent gallerist with connections to most Fortune 500 executives. Bright lights and big checks await your inevitable success. Okay, this is overstating the case, but let us be honest, every artist has dreams of this happening. The reality is much different. I compare this to the young lawyer dreaming of joining a law firm partnership. Once again, bright lights and big checks will fall into the young lawyer's lap. I discovered that this was not the case when I joined a legal partnership. My reality was as far from that happy scenario as you can imagine.

Let us assume that you need a longer learning curve to reach a point when a prominent gallery is ready to take you on. What then? You will need to take on the mantel as a self-promoting artist without a gallery to do it for you. Again, I am assuming way too much about galleries. Very few are going to carry you along. There is a strong case against using galleries, and in this chapter, we will look at five good arguments against a gallery representing you. The five reasons why a gallery may be the answer for you.

1. Higher Commission Rates: Galleries typically charge 40-50% commission rates on each sale, which can significantly reduce the artist's profit margins. Also, this means a higher price for your art, which may slow down sales to a trickle or dry them up entirely. If you sell your work, you get to keep more; potentially, your sales can multiply due to affordability.

2. Loss of Creative Control: When working with a gallery, artists may have to compromise on the presentation, pricing, and marketing of their work, potentially limiting their creative control. If you are a "controlling" type, as many solo entrepreneurs are, then this could be a big factor. You do not want to be checking up on your gallery owner every week. Getting into arguments

over how your work is presented can also grow tiresome very quickly for both of you.

3. Dependence on the Gallery: Artists may become too reliant on the gallery for sales and exposure, leading to a lack of diversification in their marketing strategies. I see this often. The artist does very little to build their career. They check out and leave it all to the gallery. The gallery, in turn, has many other artists to think about, too. What happens when the gallery declines more paintings from you because you are not actively helping to build your brand and indirectly, your sales? You will be left at a big disadvantage without building your marketing chops. These days galleries expect their artists to get involved in promoting their work and directing more eyes to the gallery.

4. Limited Flexibility: Galleries often have specific requirements and formats for showcasing art, limiting the artist's ability to experiment with new styles or mediums. You may get around this issue by researching and approaching galleries that show the type of work you produce. However, if your gallery starts to lean towards new genres, mediums, and styles of work, you could find that your artwork is no longer viewed with favor. It will be time to move on or change your style to follow the trend.

5. Marketing and Advertising Costs: Artists may need to pay for their own marketing and advertising efforts, or at least contribute, which can be expensive and time-consuming. If you will do this, then why not go it alone? You need to consider these questions and honestly assess your skills, motivations, and vision for your future.

The argument in favor of gallery representation:

6. Time-Consuming and Resource-Intensive: Managing a solo career requires significant time and resources, which can be challenging for artists who are already busy creating art. As mentioned in this book, business can take up to eighty percent of your time. If you do not love that process, then get help. A gallery can help take the load off your shoulders. Please note, however, that many galleries do not do much to promote individual artists. I get this, too. A

gallery runs very differently than a solo entrepreneur bootstrapping their way along. The gallery owner may be exhausted from taking care of the many issues of running a bricks and mortar store. They then feel that once the doors open at 10 am each day, they can sit back and let the punters walk in alone. Therefore, select the right gallery for you so that you can relax knowing that they are promoting your work.

7. Limited Exposure: Artists may struggle to reach a broader audience and gain exposure to new collectors and markets without a gallery. A successful gallerist will have contacts, which alone could see you get sales. The gallery needs feet through the door, and we must assume that they will help and encourage more viewers. Indeed, seeing art in person is still the best way to conclude a sale.

8. Difficulty in Building a Reputation: Solo artists may find it more difficult to establish a reputation and build a loyal client base without the backing of a reputable gallery. This is human nature. If you see an artist represented in a nice gallery, you will hold that artist's work in higher esteem. That may not be fair, but it is true.

9. Difficulty in Negotiating Prices: Artists may struggle to negotiate prices for their work without the leverage and expertise of a gallery. The gallery knows the market in its town and the popular styles and genres. They know market values through sheer experience and can provide an objective assessment. Something we artists struggle to do with our own work. You can learn a lot about pricing art from a gallery.

10. Difficulty in Managing Sales and Logistics: Solo artists may need to handle sales, shipping, and other logistical tasks, which can be time-consuming and distracting from their creative work. I can confirm that the worst part about selling art is packaging and shipping. Artists loathe this aspect of the process even when they should be overjoyed with the sale. This can be made simpler by being prepared with correct-sized boxes and packaging materials. Also, a relationship with a reputable courier is easy enough to develop. Keep in mind that the cheapest is not always the best.

These points suggest drawbacks and plusses that are worth thinking about. Once you have considered your circumstances you will have a better idea of which option you want to take.

Best of Both Worlds: Gallery and Solo Seller

Well, look at that. Not only does a gallery represent you, but you also have a knack for marketing. You have a following that happily purchases your art directly from your studio. Nice, but keep these points in mind to maintain a healthy and productive relationship with the gallery:

1. Communication:

Ensure that both parties have a clear understanding of the relationship's terms, including the commission rates, sales expectations, and any other terms. The latter can include issues like contacting collectors, what type of paintings you sell compared to those in the gallery, and marketing costs.

- Regularly discuss and confirm all aspects of the relationship to avoid misunderstandings.

2. Studio Sales:

If the artist has a sole agency contract, be clear about studio sales and ensure that the gallery is aware of any direct sales to friends and family. Discuss and agree on the terms of studio sales to avoid any potential conflicts.

3. Artwork Condition:

Ensure that all artwork delivered to the gallery is in exhibition condition, framed and ready to hang unless agreed otherwise.

4. Feedback and Guidance:

Be open to feedback from the gallery that can increase the saleability or quality of the artwork. Respond constructively to any suggestions or criticisms from the gallery to maintain a positive and collaborative relationship.

5. Marketing and Promotion:

Understand how the gallery promotes the artist's work and ensure that both parties are aligned on marketing strategies. Galleries mostly favor the artist doing their marketing and brand building. You will, however, need to avoid conflicting with the gallery or, in some way, drawing potential buyers away from the gallery to your studio. Common sense should determine what is fair or not.

6. Respect and Trust:

Maintain a professional and respectful attitude toward the gallery, recognizing its value in terms of exposure and sales. Trust the gallery to handle sales and logistics and avoid competing with them directly. Respect their clients and never try to lure gallery clients away to your studio. If a gallery client innocently approaches you directly, you should refer them back to the gallery. If you sell directly to that client, it must be done with the gallery's consent, and you should reach an agreement on commission sharing. If not, you have to pay the entire commission to the gallery.

7. Flexibility and Adaptability:

Be prepared to adapt to changes in the market, sales trends, or the gallery's needs. Be flexible in pricing, presentation, and other relationship aspects to ensure mutual success. You are in a type of partnership where utmost trust and moral dealing are paramount. If the gallery fails you, iron out the issue or terminate the relationship. Expect the gallery to work the same way with you.

By focusing on these key points, artists can maintain a strong and productive relationship with their gallery, ensuring a successful and sustainable career in the art world.

Ideas and Resources for Side-Hustle Success

What follows are side hustle ideas that have been successfully tried by many other artists. I cannot say whether you and any of the ideas are a good fit. You will read the list, and no doubt, a few ideas will spring out to you and say, "Try me!" That may be your intuition talking. It may be the sandwich you had for tea. However, I suggest that your creative intuition is signaling a possible fit. Explore the idea further with the recommended resources as well. Have fun. Who knows where they may lead you?

Here are twenty side hustle ideas for artists working with paint, ink, pen, pencil, and similar media, along with suggestions for websites and marketplaces to help you market your work:

Side Hustle Ideas:

1. **Custom Portraits**: Create personalized portraits of people or pets. Market through Etsy, Fiverr, or your own website.

2. **Commissions**: You can take custom requests for specific artwork pieces. To showcase your work, you can use Instagram, DeviantArt, and personal websites.

3. **Art Prints**: Sell prints of your original artwork. Use Printful, Society6, or Redbubble. These are print-on-demand sites. If you want to sell your prints out of hand, you may need to work closely with a local printer to correctly color map your art. Prints look different from the image on your computer or phone. Getting a satisfactory print entails some testing.

4. **Greeting Cards**: Design and sell unique greeting cards for various occasions. Market through Etsy or local craft fairs. Analog still has a place.

5. **Illustrations for Books**: Provide illustrations for self-published authors or small publishing houses. Advertise on Upwork, Fiverr, or LinkedIn. You still cannot beat working with a real person, despite what AI fans say.

6. **Art Classes/Workshops**: Offer online or in-person art classes and workshops. Use platforms like Skillshare, Udemy, or local community centers. This is important as it is a true passive income generator.

7. **Murals and Wall Art**: Paint murals for homes or businesses. Market through local business networks, Instagram, and your website.

8. **Freelance Graphic Design**: Offer design services for logos, branding, or marketing materials. Use Fiverr, Upwork, or 99designs.

9. **Art Licensing**: License your art for use on products like calendars, clothing, or home decor. Use sites like ArtLicensing.com.

10. **Tattoo Design**: Create custom tattoo designs. Market through Instagram, local tattoo shops, or platforms like Etsy.

11. **Art Subscription Boxes**: Create a subscription service where subscribers receive a new piece of art monthly. Use Cratejoy or your own website.

12. **Art Blogs and Tutorials**: Start a blog or YouTube channel with art tutorials and tips, monetized through ads and sponsorships. It takes a little while to get monetized, but it will happen.

13. **Art for Events:** Create custom artwork for weddings, birthdays, or corporate events. Market through event planning websites and local business networks.

14. **Print-on-Demand Products**: Create designs for print-on-demand products like t-shirts, mugs, and phone cases. Use sites like Teespring, Merch by Amazon, or Redbubble. Marketing is super important for this to work as the barrier to entry is so low.

15. **Sell on Social Media**: Use Instagram, Facebook, and Pinterest to sell your art directly to followers. Thrift sites on Instagram and Facebook marketplace are always looking for small, affordable artworks too.

16. **Art Exhibitions**: Host small exhibitions or art shows locally, charging an entry fee or selling your art directly. Collaborate with other artists for a special event. Charge per stall?

17. **Art Therapy Sessions**: Offer art therapy sessions (if qualified) to help individuals express themselves creatively. Market through local health and wellness centers.

18. **Collaborations with Brands**: Partner with brands to create limited-edition products or designs. Reach out to companies directly or use platforms like Collabor8.

19. **Digital Downloads**: Sell digital versions of your artwork for customers to print at home. Use Etsy or Gumroad.

20. **Illustrated Journals/Planners**: Design and sell beautifully illustrated journals or planners. Use Etsy or Kickstarter for funding and sales. Also, sell low-content books like coloring books, journals, and puzzles on Amazon KDP.

Websites and Marketplaces to Market Your Work:

1. **Etsy**: Great for selling handmade and custom items, including art prints, greeting cards, and digital downloads.

2. **Redbubble**: Ideal for selling art prints and print-on-demand products like t-shirts, mugs, and stickers.

3. **Society6**: Similar to Redbubble, this site allows you to sell your art on various products.

4. **Printful**: Integrate with your online store to sell print-on-demand products with your designs.

5. **Fiverr**: Offer services like custom portraits, tattoo designs, and freelance graphic design.

6. **Upwork**: Find freelance jobs for illustration, graphic design, and other art-related projects.

7. **Skillshare/Udemy**: Platforms to offer and market online art classes and tutorials.

8. **Instagram**: Showcase and sell your art to followers using features like Instagram Shopping.

9. **DeviantArt**: Share your art, gain a following, and potentially sell prints and commissions.

10. **ArtLicensing.com**: License your artwork for use on various products.

11. **99designs**: Participate in design contests or offer your graphic design services.

12. **Pinterest** Market to people who are likely to be interested in creative work.

13. **Cratejoy**: Create and market your art subscription box.

14. **YouTube**: Start a channel for art tutorials and monetize through ads and sponsorships. Just start. Monetize later, but begin.

15. **Gumroad**: Sell digital downloads and tutorials directly to customers. This is a solid platform if you do not have your own shopping platform. It is free and growing constantly.

16. **Teespring**: Design and sell custom apparel and accessories.

17. **Merch by Amazon**: Sell your designs on Amazon's print-on-demand platform.

18. **Amazon KDP; Draft to Digital and Blurb**: These platforms allow you to sell your books, journals and instructional books.

19. **Kickstarter**: Fund and launch unique art projects or products.

20. **Collabor8**: Find and collaborate with brands for special projects and limited editions.

These ideas and platforms can help you leverage your creative skills to generate additional income while maintaining the security of a day job. Persist, have fun, and Good luck!

Smart Ways to Reduce Costs

Transitioning from a side-hustle to a full-time art career can be challenging, especially when it comes to managing your finances. In this chapter, we will explore some smart strategies that artists can implement to reduce costs at various stages of their careers. 1. Cost-Saving Strategies for Side-Hustle Artists As a side-hustle artist, it's important to make the most of your limited resources. Here are some cost-saving strategies to consider: Utilize Free and Low-Cost Marketing Tools: In today's digital age, social media platforms have become powerful tools for artists to showcase their work and connect with potential buyers. Platforms like Instagram, Facebook, and Pinterest can help you reach a wider audience without having to spend a fortune on marketing. Additionally, email marketing can be an effective way to keep your audience informed and engaged. Take advantage of free email marketing services like Mailchimp for small lists. These services offer basic features that can help you stay connected with your followers without breaking the bank. Creating an online portfolio is essential for any artist looking to establish themselves in the art world. Instead of investing in expensive website builders, start with affordable options like Wix, Squarespace, or WordPress using free themes. These platforms provide user-friendly templates that allow you to showcase your artwork professionally. Art Materials: When it comes to art materials, there are several ways you can save money: Consider negotiating discounts with suppliers by buying materials in bulk. Many art supply stores offer membership discounts or special rates for bulk orders, especially when these orders are made regularly. I seem to order art materials every month. My art supplier likes consistent orders and therefore is prepared to offer a discount. You can take advantage of these opportunities whenever possible.

Another cost-saving strategy is to team up with other local artists to make group purchases of art supplies. By buying in bulk together, you can take advantage of discounts and share the cost savings among yourselves.

If you have a platform like a YouTube channel, you may receive free materials to review from time to time. This is inconsistent, but we never turn our nose up on free art supplies. Never!

You may even ask for samples to review. Most stores receive many free samples from art supply representatives. Why would they not give a few to their favorite artist (you) for a review and a shoutout on social media? Thrift stores can be treasure troves for artists on a budget. Look out for old frames you can refurbish instead of buying new ones at higher prices. This saves money and adds character and uniqueness to your artwork. Think outside the box when it comes to sourcing materials. Consider using found objects or recycled materials to create your art. Not only is this an eco-friendly approach, but it also reduces the need to buy new supplies constantly. Collaborate and Trade Skills: Collaboration is key in the art world. By trading your art or skills with other professionals, you can save money on services essential for your career growth. Consider exchanging your artwork for graphic design, marketing, or photography services. This skill exchange not only helps you save money but also allows you to build a network of like-minded individuals who can support and promote your work. By implementing these smart strategies, side hustle artists can reduce costs while pursuing their artistic passions. Every penny saved is a step closer to financial stability as an artist. Managing your finances wisely becomes even more crucial as you continue on your artistic journey and transition into a full-time career.

Cost Saving on Transition

As an artist who is considering transitioning from a hobbyist to selling your art, it's important to understand the financial implications and find ways to cut costs without compromising the quality of your work. In this chapter, we will explore various cost-saving strategies that can help you make this transition smoothly. Marketing: One of the key aspects of selling your art is marketing yourself effectively. However, hiring professional marketers can be costly, especially if you're just starting out. Instead, consider taking a DIY approach to marketing. There are numerous free online courses and resources available that can help you learn basic marketing skills. By investing time in learning these skills, you can promote your art without breaking the bank. Additionally, reach out to local media outlets such as newspapers, blogs, and community websites. Many of them are often looking for interesting stories or features on local artists. By getting your work featured in these publications, you can gain exposure and attract potential buyers without spending a dime on advertising. Art Materials: Art supplies can quickly become expensive if you're not careful. To save money on materials, consider joining wholesale clubs or art supply co-ops. These organizations offer discounted prices on art supplies for their members. By purchasing materials from them instead of regular retail stores, you can significantly reduce your expenses. Another cost-saving strategy is to look for secondhand art supplies through online marketplaces or local art schools. Many artists sell or donate their unused materials at a fraction of the original price. It's worth exploring these options as you may find high-quality materials at affordable prices. Framing and Presentation: Proper framing and presentation enhance the overall appeal of your artwork but can be an expensive endeavor if done professionally for each piece. Instead of relying solely on professional framers, consider learning how to frame your own work using materials from thrift stores or buying framing kits. Thrift stores often have frames in various sizes and styles at affordable prices. With a little bit of creativity, you can repurpose these frames to suit your artwork. Alternatively, framing kits are available at reasonable prices and come with all the necessary materials and instructions. By taking the DIY approach to framing, you can save a significant amount of money without compromising on the final presentation. Financial Management: Transitioning from an art hobbyist to selling your work requires careful financial management. Creating a detailed budget is crucial in tracking your expenses and identifying areas where you can cut costs. Start by listing all your art-related expenses, including materials, marketing efforts, framing supplies, exhibition fees, etc. Having this information in front of you will give you a clear overview of where your money is going and help you make informed decisions about reducing costs. Furthermore, keeping detailed records of all your art-related expenses can potentially benefit you during tax season. By organizing receipts and invoices for purchases related to your art business, you may be eligible for tax deductions. Consult with a tax professional or research the specific guidelines in your country to ensure compliance with tax regulations. Transitioning from an art hobbyist to selling your work requires careful consideration of finances. By implementing cost-saving strategies such as DIY marketing techniques, joining wholesale clubs for discounted materials, learning how to frame your own work using thrift store finds or framing kits, creating a detailed budget to track expenses efficiently while maximizing potential tax deductions; artists can successfully navigate this transition without breaking the bank.

Saving Costs as a Full Time Artist

As an artist, managing your finances is crucial, especially when you decide to pursue art as a full-time career. In this chapter, we will explore various cost-saving strategies to help you navigate the financial challenges of being a professional artist. One area where artists can save money is in marketing. Content marketing is an effective way to attract and engage an audience. By creating valuable content such as blog posts, video tutorials, or behind-the-scenes looks at your process, you can establish yourself as an authority in your field and generate interest in your artwork. This organic approach to marketing not only saves money but also builds a loyal following that can lead to increased sales. Another cost-effective marketing tool is email campaigns. We have covered this to a degree already. However, you now need to use that marketing opportunity. You can drive sales and increase engagement by nurturing relationships with your audience through targeted email campaigns. These campaigns allow you to stay connected with your patrons and inform them about new artwork releases or upcoming exhibitions without spending a fortune on traditional advertising methods. A weekly email is not excessive. Once a month may be too seldom. Yes, it is possible to become a stranger, and this can lead to your subscriber unsubscribing.

On the subject of email marketing, try to use a dedicated email marketing platform rather than something like Gmail. There are many reasons for this, which I cover in detail in my book The Art of Content Marketing. You can find email platforms for a once-off price, too, which saves on expensive subscriptions. This will be money well spent. Art materials are another significant expense for artists. Building solid relationships with art suppliers can help negotiate better deals and discounts on materials. Reach out to local suppliers and explore opportunities for collaboration that benefit both parties involved. Also, could you consider applying for artist residencies that provide materials and workspace at reduced costs or even for free? These residencies offer financial relief and opportunities for artistic growth and networking within the art community. Take a look at Artwork Archive for the listing of artist residencies.

Framing: Framing and presentation are essential aspects of showcasing your artwork professionally but can be costly. To save money on framing expenses, consider framing multiple pieces simultaneously to take advantage of bulk discounts from framers. This approach allows you to negotiate better deals while maintaining consistency in the presentation of your work. I had a framer make many frames of a similar size so that I could pop in a painting anytime. If traditional framing proves too expensive, explore alternative display methods such as mounting artwork on boards or using clip frames. These options are often more affordable while still providing a professional presentation for your artwork.

Many artists sell their work unframed, too. This can save the buyer costs and allow the buyer to get a frame to their personal tastes. Box canvasses can remain unframed for a minimalist look. There are many variables these days. If you are sending work overseas, then unframed is a good option. Shipping cost savings will often cover the cost of a new frame. Pass this saving on to the buyer, and it can close a sale for you.

Finally, you can consider opening your framing studio. I was able to do this when a friend mentioned to me that a framing company had second-hand framing equipment for sale. The equipment belonged to a deceased estate. I purchased a guillotine and underpinner for excellent prices. These two items are the workhorses of a framing studio. I have ramed hundreds of paintings over the years since, and this has saved me many thousands in costs.

Professional help is sometimes necessary for artists, but it doesn't have to break the bank. Bartering services with professionals who can assist you with accounting, legal advice, or marketing can be a cost-effective solution. You create a mutually beneficial arrangement that helps both parties save money by exchanging your artistic skills for their expertise. Consider hiring interns or part-time assistants from local art schools. If Jeff Koons can use art workers, then why not you? These individuals can help with administrative tasks, production, or marketing in exchange for experience and mentorship. It's a win-win situation as they gain valuable knowledge while supporting your artistic endeavors. Building a strong community and support network is vital for artists. Joining or forming artist collectives allows you to share resources, studio space, and even marketing efforts. By pooling your resources together, you can reduce overhead costs and benefit from collective marketing initiatives that reach a wider audience. Offering workshops and classes is another way to supplement your income while offsetting costs. Sharing your skills and expertise generates additional revenue and establishes you as an expert in your field. This increased visibility can lead to new opportunities and further financial stability. Implementing these cost-saving strategies into your art career can help you effectively manage your finances during different stages of development. Adopting these practices ensures a more sustainable and successful transition into full-time artistry, whether you are just starting out or have been working as an artist for years. Remember that being mindful of expenses doesn't mean compromising your artwork's quality but finding creative solutions that allow you to thrive as an artist without unnecessary financial burden.

Getting Organized: Record Keeping

Proper record-keeping is crucial for managing your art business efficiently. Keeping track of sales, expenses, and artwork details not only helps you stay organized but also ensures you are prepared for tax time. In this chapter, we will explore strategies and tools to help you streamline your record-keeping process. One effective way to simplify your record-keeping is by linking your bank accounts with financial software. This integration allows for automatic updates and categorization of transactions, reducing the need for manual data entry. There are several recommended software options available: (some links and resources at the end of the book) 1. QuickBooks: Widely used by small businesses, QuickBooks offers features such as expense tracking, invoicing, and tax preparation. 2. Xero: Known for its user-friendly interface, Xero provides comprehensive accounting features and real-time financial data. 3. Wave: A free accounting software ideal for artists, Wave includes features for invoicing, expense tracking, and receipt scanning. The benefits of using financial software linked to your bank accounts are numerous. Transactions are automatically imported and categorized in real time. This allows you to keep track of your financial health at a glance while simplifying tax filing by organizing your financial data and generating necessary reports. I admit that I was highly skeptical of this linking system. I thought I would be hacked and cammed, and all those stories would happen to me. Many years later, I can say that the linking system has saved me untold hours of work. Not to mention the stress avoided too. In addition to managing sales and expenses, it is essential to have a system in place for you to track your artwork inventory. Art inventory management systems can help you keep detailed records of each piece of art, including creation dates, dimensions used, materials, pricing history, and sales information. Three recommended systems that can assist in this process are: 1. Artwork Archive: This comprehensive tool offers features such as tracking artwork inventory, managing sales contacts, and generating reports. 2.Art Galleria: This service is designed specifically for managing art collections galleries and provides services like inventory management,sales tracking,and reporting. 3.ArtMoi : A cost-effective solution that enables artists to catalog their work and manage sales records. Setting up an organized record-keeping system is crucial for your financial records and art inventory. Here are some critical steps to follow: 1. Organize Financial Records: - Track all sources of income, including art sales, commissions, and teaching fees. - Categorize expenses such as materials, studio rent, marketing, travel, and professional services. Keeping your private and business records separate is a pain but necessary. - Keep digital copies of all receipts and invoices for easy access and organization. 2. Maintain an Art Inventory: - Record information about each piece of artwork, including title, dimensions, medium used, and date of creation. - Document the sale date, buyer's information, sale price, and any related expenses or commissions. - Keep track of where each piece is located, whether it's in your studio, on consignment, or sold. 3. Generate and Store Documents: Utilize your inventory management system to generate important documents such as consignment records,sales agreements,and certificates of authenticity. - Ensure all documents are easily accessible and regularly backed up. When tax season arrives, it is essential to be prepared. Having organized financial data will make this process much smoother. You can use your financial software to generate profit and loss statements, expense reports, and income summaries. These reports will enable you to complete your tax filings accurately and efficiently. In addition, working with a professional such as an accountant or bookkeeper familiar with the art industry may be beneficial. They can help you navigate tax regulations, maximize deductions, and ensure your financial records are well-organized and accessible. All of this takes time to set up, but it will be worth it before your first trading year is over.

Legal and Financial Issues for Selling Art

When selling your art, there are several important legal and financial considerations to remember to ensure that your business is compliant, protected, and financially sound. Please keep in mind that this book is aimed at exploring the idea of selling your art. This is not legal or financial advice; therefore, please ensure that you first get the appropriate advice from a certified professional. With that said here's a breakdown of these considerations:

Legal Considerations

1. Business Structure

Choose a Business Entity:

- Decide whether you will operate as a sole proprietor, LLC (Limited Liability Company), or corporation. Each structure has different implications for liability, taxes, and administrative requirements.

- An LLC can provide personal liability protection without the complexity of a corporation. Talk to your accountant about these options. A common mistake is to wait too long to do this. You want to see how things turn out before taking the big step and getting corporations registered. Yes you do have some leeway (that is not meant to be a legal term) where the line between hobby and professional is blurred. When you see that you are going ahead with your business then get the paperwork out of the way.

2. Contracts and Agreements

Sales Contracts:

• Use contracts for the sale of your art to outline the terms, including payment, delivery, and return policies. This protects both you and the buyer. In short, put everything in writing.

Commission Agreements:

• If you accept commissions, have an explicit agreement that outlines the scope of work, deadlines, payment terms, and rights to the artwork. You can find commission template agreements online too. It is a starting point, and you may need to iron the terms out. Consult your attorney.

Gallery Agreements:

• When working with galleries, have a formal agreement that details the commission rate, payment schedule, and responsibilities for marketing and shipping.

3. Intellectual Property

Copyright:

• Understand your rights regarding the copyright of your artwork. You retain the copyright even after selling an original piece unless you explicitly transfer it.

Licensing:

• Consider licensing your artwork for reproduction on products or commercial use. Ensure licensing agreements are clear about the scope and duration of use.

4. Taxes

Sales Tax:

● Determine if you need to collect sales tax on your artwork sales. This varies by location and the nature of your sales (e.g., in-state vs. out-of-state).

● Register for a sales tax permit if required in your jurisdiction.

Income Tax:

● Report all income from art sales on your tax return. Depending on your business structure, this could be on your personal tax return or a separate business return. Have your accountant prepare this for you to ensure you are up to date with the laws and that you are not leaving out deductions.

Estimated Taxes:

● ANother detail your accountant will clarify with you.

Financial Considerations

1. Pricing Your Art

Research:

● Research the market to price your artwork appropriately. Consider factors like the cost of materials, your time, market demand, and comparable artist prices.

Consistency:

● Maintain consistent pricing across different platforms and galleries to build trust and avoid buyer confusion.

2. Record Keeping

Track Income and Expenses:

● Keep detailed records of all your art sales, income, and expenses. This is crucial for tax purposes and understanding your business's financial health.

Software Solutions:

● Use accounting software like QuickBooks, FreshBooks, or Wave to track your finances, link bank accounts, and generate financial reports.

3. Budgeting

Operational Costs:

● Create a budget for your art business, including materials, marketing, shipping, studio rent, and other overhead costs.

Profit Margin:

● Ensure that your pricing covers your costs and includes a profit margin to sustain your business.

4. Insurance

Business Insurance:

● Consider getting business insurance that covers your art studio, artwork, liability, and any employees you might have.

Health and Disability Insurance:

● As a self-employed artist, look into health and disability insurance to protect yourself from unforeseen medical expenses and loss of income due to injury or illness.

Additional Considerations

1. Shipping and Handling

Shipping Costs:

- Include shipping costs in your pricing or clearly communicate them to buyers. Consider offering insured shipping to protect against loss or damage.

Packaging:

- Invest in quality packaging materials to ensure your artwork arrives safely. Include instructions for handling and care. It is funny to me how my approach has changed over the years. When I first started selling across the country and had to package the paintings, I made my own boxes. Often, I still do because box size directly relates to the price of shipping. I can now make a box that looks pretty darn professional. My first attempts were not that great though. Never skimp on materials that protect the painting, especially if it is framed. Sponge foam to cushion the frame is advised to prevent damage. Price these items into your expenses as they add up, but it is better to be safe than sorry, so do not cut corners.

Conclusion

Navigating the legal and financial aspects of selling your art can be complex, but it is essential for building a sustainable and professional art business. By setting up the right business structure, using contracts, protecting your intellectual property, and maintaining meticulous financial records, you can protect your interests and focus more on your creative process. Consider consulting with legal and financial professionals to tailor these considerations to your specific situation.

How to Protect Your Art

Protecting your art legally involves several steps to safeguard your intellectual property, manage your business relationships, and ensure your rights are upheld. Here are the necessary steps to take:

1. Understand and Use Copyright Laws

Copyright Basics

- **Automatic Protection:** In many jurisdictions, your artwork is automatically protected by copyright as soon as it is created and fixed in a tangible form (e.g., canvas, digital file).

- **Exclusive Rights:** Copyright gives you the exclusive right to reproduce, distribute, display, perform, and create derivative works based on your art.

Registration

- **Formal Registration:** While copyright is automatic, registering your work with the relevant government authority (e.g., the U.S. Copyright Office) provides additional legal benefits, such as the ability to sue for statutory damages and attorney's fees in case of infringement.

- **Proof of Ownership:** Registration establishes a public record of your copyright and can serve as proof of ownership in disputes.

2. Use Watermarks and Digital Protections

Watermarks

- **Visibility:** Adding watermarks to your digital images can deter unauthorized use. Ensure the watermark is noticeable but not too obtrusive. I prefer an attractive logo.

- **Consistent Branding:** Use your name or logo to help with brand recognition and protection. This makes more sense to me as it is your brand. Get a good logo early on in your business. It is far more attractive to subtly brand your posts, for example, than to place an unsightly watermark across the middle of your photographs. That is most annoying to the viewer.

Metadata

- **Embed Metadata:** Add metadata to your digital files, including your name, copyright notice, and contact information. This can help track and prove ownership if the image is misused.

3. Licensing and Usage Agreements

Licensing

- **Clear Terms:** When licensing your artwork for reproduction or commercial use, use clear, written agreements that specify the scope, duration, and terms of use.

- **Types of Licenses:** Decide whether to grant exclusive or non-exclusive licenses and detail any restrictions on how the artwork can be used.

Usage Agreements

- **Commission Contracts:** For commissioned works, use contracts that outline the terms, including payment, deadlines, and rights to the artwork.

- **Gallery Agreements:** When exhibiting in galleries, have formal agreements detailing commission rates, display duration, and responsibilities for marketing and shipping.

4. Trademark Your Brand

Logo and Brand Name

- **Trademark Protection:** If you have a distinctive logo, brand name, or tagline associated with your art business, consider registering them as trademarks. This protects your brand identity and prevents others from using similar marks.

5. Monitor and Enforce Your Rights

Online Monitoring

- **Image Searches:** Use reverse image search tools like Google Images or TinEye to find unauthorized uses of your artwork online.

- **Monitoring Services:** Consider using services that specialize in monitoring the use of your images and alerting you to potential infringements.

Take Action Against Infringement

- **Cease and Desist:** If you discover unauthorized use of your artwork, send a cease and desist letter to the infringer, demanding that they stop using your work and compensate you if necessary.

- **Legal Action:** If the infringement continues or causes significant harm, consider taking legal action. Consult an intellectual property attorney to discuss your options and the potential for litigation.

6. Protect Your Work Physically

Physical Security

- **Secure Storage:** Ensure your physical artworks are stored securely to prevent theft or damage.

- **Insurance:** Insure your artwork against loss, theft, and damage. This can include studio insurance and transit insurance for when your work is being shipped or displayed.

7. Business Practices

Record Keeping

- **Document Creation:** Keep detailed records of your artwork, including photographs, descriptions, creation dates, and any sales or licenses. This documentation can be crucial in proving ownership and the originality of your work. Even online posts can be a record of when the artwork first appeared.

- **Sales and Contracts:** Maintain copies of all sales receipts, contracts, and correspondence related to your artwork.

Professional Advice

- **Consult Professionals:** Regularly consult with legal and financial professionals to ensure your practices are up-to-date and compliant with current laws.

Conclusion

Protecting your art legally involves a combination of proactive measures and vigilant monitoring. By understanding and leveraging copyright laws, using watermarks and metadata, establishing clear licensing agreements, and trademarking your brand, you can safeguard your intellectual property. Additionally, monitoring for infringement and maintaining thorough records will help you enforce your rights effectively. Consulting with legal professionals can provide further tailored advice and support in protecting your creative work.

Finding Time to Paint Despite Business Demands

Balancing time between art and business is a common challenge for artists, especially when business tasks like marketing, content creation, and teaching take up a significant portion of your time. Here are strategies to help you optimize your schedule, making the most of the time you have for painting and ensuring your art practice flourishes:

1. Time Management Techniques

Prioritize and Schedule

Set Clear Priorities:

- Identify your top priorities each week for both business and art. Determine which tasks are most critical to your success and allocate time accordingly.

Block Scheduling:

- Use block scheduling to allocate specific times of the day or week for different activities. For instance, designate mornings for painting and afternoons for business tasks.

Daily and Weekly Planning

Daily Schedule:

- Start each day with a clear plan. List your tasks and allocate specific times for each, ensuring you dedicate at least a portion of your day to painting.

Weekly Review:

- Review your weekly schedule and adjust as needed. Ensure that you're consistently setting aside time for art, even if it means shifting other tasks.

2. Delegation and Outsourcing

Hire Help

Administrative Tasks:

- Consider hiring an assistant for administrative tasks like managing emails, scheduling, and bookkeeping. This can free up significant time for you to focus on painting. If you cannot bring yourself to do this, invest in software that simplifies these tasks.

Marketing and Content Creation:

- Outsource social media management, content creation, and website maintenance tasks to professionals or freelancers. If this is still beyond your budget or you are a control freak like me, consider using a scheduling software like Buffer to schedule your posts well in advance. Scheduling is the secret power of efficient creators.

Collaborate

Team Up:

- Collaborate with other artists or business professionals who can share the workload. This can include joint marketing efforts, shared studio space, or co-teaching classes.

3. Efficient Business Practices

Automation

Tools and Software:

• Use automation tools to handle repetitive tasks. Email marketing services, social media schedulers, and accounting software can save you hours each week.

Templates and Systems:

• Create templates for frequently used documents like invoices, contracts, and emails. Establish systems and workflows to streamline your business processes.

Batch Processing

Batch Tasks:

• Batch similar tasks together to improve efficiency. For example, dedicate one day a week to creating and scheduling all your social media content.

4. Set Boundaries

Work-Life Balance

Office Hours:

• Set specific "office hours" for business tasks and stick to them. This helps prevent business activities from encroaching on your creative time.

Non-Negotiable Art Time:

• Treat your painting time as a non-negotiable appointment. Schedule it in your calendar and protect it like any other important meeting. If you want to be treated like a professional then you will need to act like and demand that others respect that. Of course, you want to remain the kind and mindful person you have always been, but there are limits.

5. Maximize Painting Efficiency

Focused Studio Time

Prepare Ahead:

- Prepare your studio the night before to maximize your painting time. Have your materials ready so you can start working immediately. Clean your brushes at the end of the day. Tidy up. Clean out garbage bins filled with bad-smelling rags, old paint, or whatever. Those things can be toxic.

Minimize Distractions:

- Create a distraction-free environment when painting. Turn off notifications and set boundaries with family and friends during art time. TIP: It is nice to make your space attractive. This often starts with a regular decluttering program. Sure, the stereotypical artist is untidy, and the studio looks like an abstract expressionist's nightmare, but hey, a tidy studio means you get things done easier. I do a declutter about three times a year. I hate doing it, but I love the result. Yes, being an artist is weird, but I would not change it for the world.

Short Sessions

Quick Studies:

- Utilize short, focused painting sessions if your schedule is tight. Even 30 minutes of dedicated painting time can be productive.

Sketches and Preparatory Work:

- Work on sketches, studies, or preparatory pieces during shorter time slots. This keeps you engaged with your art even on busy days.

6. Integrate Art and Business

Content Creation

Process Sharing:

- Share your creative process as part of your content creation. This not only markets your work but also keeps you engaged in your art during business tasks.

Educational Content:

- Use your art practice as material for teaching content. Record your painting sessions for online classes or create tutorials based on your work. By using your recordings for multiple purposes, you get so much done. Repurpose content is a popular catchphrase for this idea. We artists have tons of content already recorded and photographed. Rework it. You will be surprised with the results. Try apps like Canva, free, and discover many ways with a single photograph.

Conclusion

Balancing time between art and business requires intentional planning, efficient practices, and sometimes seeking help. By prioritizing your tasks, delegating where possible, and creating boundaries, you can ensure that your painting time is protected and productive. Remember that the quality of your creative time matters as much as the quantity, so make every painting session count.

Remember Why You Did This: Your Higher Purpose

As you transition into a part-time or full-time career, it is crucial to remember why you chose this path in the first place. Beyond financial goals, pursuing art often stems from a desire to relax, have fun, and live a purposeful life. In this chapter, we will explore tips and strategies to ensure that artists maintain a healthy balance, avoid burnout, and continue finding joy in their creative endeavors. Reconnecting with Your Core Motivations: It is essential for you to reconnect with their core motivations. Let your passion and love for creativity guide you as you navigate your artistic journey. Explore new exciting techniques and subjects, keeping your artistic pursuits fresh and inspiring. Reflect on the deeper purpose behind your art. Whether it is expressing yourself, communicating a message, or bringing beauty into the world, let this purpose be your guiding light. Engage in projects that align with your values and create a sense of fulfillment. Maintaining a Healthy Work-Life Balance: Setting boundaries between work time and personal time is crucial for maintaining a healthy work-life balance. Designate specific hours for creating art and stick to them. Avoid overworking by setting realistic goals and knowing when to take breaks. Prioritizing self-care is equally important. Please ensure you have time for relaxation, hobbies, and activities that rejuvenate you. This could involve spending time with family, practicing mindfulness or enjoying nature. Regular physical activity, healthy eating habits, and adequate sleep are essential for maintaining energy levels and focus. Embracing a Holistic Approach to Your Career: Diversifying income sources can help reduce financial pressure as an artist. Consider teaching workshops or classes related to your craft or exploring commissions or merchandise sales opportunities. This approach not only stabilizes finances but also keeps work varied and interesting. Investing in your artistic development is another way to maintain balance. Attend workshops, take courses, and experiment with new mediums. Lifelong learning keeps your skills sharp and enthusiasm high. Surrounding yourself with a supportive community of fellow artists, mentors, and friends is crucial. Share experiences, seek advice, and celebrate successes together. Collaboration and networking can provide new opportunities and reduce feelings of isolation. Strategies to

Reduce Overwork and Stress: Effective time management is key to avoiding overwork and stress. Utilize tools like calendars, to-do lists, and project management apps to organize tasks effectively. Breaking down large projects into manageable steps can also help prevent feeling overwhelmed. Don't hesitate to seek help with tasks outside your expertise. Hiring part-time assistants or bartering services can benefit administrative work or marketing tasks. Collaborating with other artists or professionals shares the workload and brings fresh perspectives to your work. Practicing mindfulness, meditation, or yoga can help manage stress while maintaining a calm and focused mind. Incorporating short breaks into your work routine allows time for resting and recharging. If you cannot think of something mindful to do, take a walk. Walking is simple and effective. It is good for your health and your mind and lets ideas percolate. Focus on the Bigger Picture: While it is important to consider long-term goals as an artist, it is equally vital to stay flexible and open to changes along the way. Your career path may change, so you can regularly revisit and adjust your goals accordingly. Recognizing and celebrating big and small achievements is crucial for maintaining motivation throughout your artistic journey. Use these milestones as opportunities for reflection on progress made so far while setting new inspiring goals for the future. Conclusion: Pursuing an art career should be a fulfilling journey that brings joy rather than constant stress. By reconnecting with core motivations, maintaining a healthy work-life balance, embracing a holistic approach to your career, and implementing strategies to reduce overwork and stress levels—you can ensure a long-lasting career filled with creativity, joy, and fulfillment. Remember, the ultimate goal is to live a purposeful life that brings happiness to yourself and those who experience your art.

Dealing with Negative Advice

The idea of turning a hobby into a business has long sparked concerns among artists. Many fear monetizing their passion will ultimately ruin their love for it, as it transforms from a beloved pastime into an obligation. While this concern is valid, it is not always true. With the right approach and mindset, you can maintain your passion for your art while building a successful business. In this chapter, we will explore how to address the negative advice surrounding turning your hobby into a business and ensure you continue loving what you do. Before diving into strategies for maintaining your passion, let's first understand the concerns associated with turning your hobby into a business. Pros: - Passion-Driven: Doing what you love for a living can be incredibly fulfilling. It allows you to pursue your artistic endeavors wholeheartedly and make a living from it. - Intrinsic Motivation: When your work is driven by passion, you are more likely to excel and innovate in new ways. Cons: - Pressure: The need to make a profit can create stress and pressure, potentially removing the joy of creating art. Routine: Transforming your hobby into a job can make it feel like another task on your to-do list, removing the spontaneity and freshness that initially attracted you to it. Now that we have identified these concerns, let's explore some strategies for balancing passion with practicality: 1. Set Clear Boundaries: Establish clear boundaries between work hours and personal time to prevent burnout and ensure that work doesn't overshadow leisure time. Define specific working hours so that you have designated time solely devoted to running your art business. Additionally, take regular breaks throughout the day to step away from work and recharge physically and mentally. 2. Diversify Activities: Engaging in different types of projects can help keep things interesting and prevent monotony. Don't limit yourself solely to commercial projects; maintain a few personal, non-commercial projects that remind you why you fell in love with your art in the first place. Maintaining a healthy work-life balance is crucial when turning your hobby into a business: 1. Separate Work and Leisure: If possible, create a separate physical space for your art business. Having a dedicated workspace can help you mentally distinguish between work and leisure time. Additionally, manage your time effectively by utilizing tools like calendars and to-do lists to ensure that you allocate time for relaxation and other hobbies. 2. Delegate Tasks: Recognize that running an art business involves more than just creating art. Consider outsourcing administrative work, marketing, or accounting to professionals or hiring help for overwhelming tasks. Collaboration with others can also alleviate the load while introducing fresh ideas, making the business side of things less daunting. Staying connected to your passion is essential throughout this journey: 1. Regular Reflection: Regularly revisit your goals and remind yourself why you started this journey in the first place. Reflecting on your artistic vision and purpose will help you maintain enthusiasm during challenging times. Additionally, celebrate both big and small achievements along the way to stay motivated and positive. 2. Continuous Learning: Invest time learning new techniques, exploring different mediums, attending workshops and exhibitions, or engaging with other artists through online communities. Continuous learning keeps your creative skills sharp while inspiring like-minded individuals. Approaching the business side of things with a creative mindset is key: 1. Innovative Marketing: You can approach marketing and sales with the same creativity you apply to your art. Think outside the box when promoting your work and finding new audiences who appreciate what you create. 2. Sustainable Practices: Set realistic goals for your business to avoid unnecessary pressure while diversifying income sources (e.g., selling originals, prints, teaching, commissions). Multiple income streams can reduce financial stress and create a sustainable business model. 3. Perspective Shift: Instead of viewing the business aspect as a detractor from your art, try to see it as an extension of your creativity. This shift in perspective can make the business side more enjoyable and align it with your artistic vision. 4. Mindset: Embrace challenges as opportunities for growth and development. Adopting a growth mindset will help you overcome obstacles while maintaining your passion for art. Be adaptable and open to change; if one approach doesn't work, be willing to try another. Turning your hobby into a business does introduce new challenges, but it doesn't have to diminish your love for art. By setting boundaries, maintaining balance, staying connected to your passion, approaching the business side creatively, and embracing the journey itself, you can enjoy a fulfilling and sustainable art career. Remember that this is an ongoing process; continuously find ways to keep your passion alive while navigating the world of art and entrepreneurship.

Pulling It All Togeher

I started this book with my art transition story. I want to pull this entire journey together by saying that it was and still is the best thing I ever did. There are times when I look at people in their twenties and thirties and think, if only I had made this move at, say, thirty, how far would I be today? That is a futile thinking process. My life journey is not your life journey. You need to act now, but not recklessly either. Everything takes time. The proviso is that you are taking action. That you are moving forward with your plans. That your dreams are turning into reality.

Never wait until times are perfect. I tried that, but it was due to fear. There is never a perfect time. Life moves onwards, and you either take part in it or watch it go by. Keep this in mind: artists are a select few who understand they are artists. Many artists remain in a cocoon of fear and unrealized dreams. Some grow resentful and angry. Do not be that person. You will recognize these types who insult other artists living their dreams. Who try to pull down others and humiliate them. Call them delusional or foolish. These sad people are those too fearful to try. They know it, too.

Instead, live like an artist. Call yourself an artist. Do the work of an artist. Take action and follow that path to see where it leads you. You do not need to be a full-time artist to be an artist. That is something I have tried to stress in this book. You must do as you see fit. Do your art in a way that makes sense for you now. But if you have aspirations to go further with it, this book will give you direction. Go forward and make those dreams come true with determined action.

I do wish you the very best with your creative pursuits.

About the Author

I want to thank you personally for reading this book. If you have reached this far, you are in the "one percent" category of people who finish what they started. Maybe we can shift that statistic a bit higher? Thanks to your self-discipline, you have achieved much. You will enjoy your life as a creatively awakened individual.

I also want to thank all those artists who study their craft with me. Whether you are a member of my Artist's Live Channel[1], own a course, or watch my YouTube videos[2]. You are also self-disciplined and no doubt experiencing growth in your art. My best wishes to you!

Further learning:

My courses on painting fundamentals: Learn to Paint with Impact[3].

Now, then, back into the third-person:

Author: Malcolm Dewey is a South African artist and writer. He paints in a contemporary Impressionist style and mostly paints landscapes and figures. He teaches painting in various mediums, including oils, acrylics, gouache, watercolor, and pastels. Malcolm sells his works to collectors all over the world, and his gallery can be viewed at www.malcolmdeweyfineart.com[4]

Connect with Malcolm on his website to join one of his free tutorials. Also Youtube/MalcolmDewey[5]

Finally, if you enjoyed this book, please give it a review on Amazon. Thank you!

---

1. https://malcolmdeweyfineart.newzenler.com/courses/artists-live-membership

2. https://www.youtube.com/MalcolmDewey

3. https://www.malcolmdeweyfineart.com/painting-course.html

4. https://www.malcolmdeweyfineart.com/painting-secrets.html

5. https://www.youtube.com/MalcolmDewey

Links and Resources

Getting organized: Artwork Archive[1]

Book: The Art of Content Marketing[2]

Quickbooks[3]

Save on Apps: Useful apps and software with lifetime deals[4].

1. https://www.artworkarchive.com/?ref=282adc

2. https://amzn.to/4bF1HM5

3. https://quickbooks.intuit.com/za/

4. https://amzn.to/4bF1HM5

Don't miss out!

Visit the website below and you can sign up to receive emails whenever Malcolm Dewey publishes a new book. There's no charge and no obligation.

https://books2read.com/r/B-A-AMPC-HPBJD

BOOKS 2 READ

Connecting independent readers to independent writers.

Also by Malcolm Dewey

An Artist's Guide to Plein Air Painting
How to Loosen Up Your Painting
An Artist's Survival Guide
The Creative Living Book Bundle
The Art of Content Marketing
52 Weeks of Creative Living: Inspiration for Your Creative Soul
Your Artist's Voice
52 Weeks of Creative Mastery
Sell Your Art or Not?

www.ingramcontent.com/pod-product-compliance
Lightning Source LLC
Chambersburg PA
CBHW052055150726
48002CB00002B/893